Jihad in the Qur'an
The Truth from the Source

Revised and Improved Third Edition

Louay Fatoohi

Luna Plena Publishing   Birmingham

Third Edition published: July 2009

Production Reference: 1100709

First Edition published: 2002, Malaysia
Second Edition published: 2004, Malaysia

Published by:
Luna Plena Publishing
Birmingham, UK.
www.lunaplenapub.com

ISBN 978-1-906342-06-7

Cover design by:
Mawlid Design
www.mawliddesign.com

Cover image:
The image on the front cover likens the critical benefits of "jihad" to the human soul to that of water to dead land. The latter is mentioned in several Qur'anic verses that remind people of God's ability to bring them back to life on the Day of Resurrection: "Allah sends down water from the sky and revives therewith the earth after its death." (from 16.65)

About the Author

Louay Fatoohi is a British scholar who was born in Baghdad, Iraq, in 1961. He converted from Christianity to Islam in his early twenties. He obtained a BSc in Physics from the College of Sciences, University of Baghdad, in 1984. He obtained his PhD in Astronomy from the Physics Department, Durham University, in 1998.

The author of several books and over forty scientific and general articles in Arabic and English, Dr Fatoohi is particularly interested in studying historical characters and events that are mentioned in the Qur'an and comparing the Qur'anic account with the Biblical narratives, other Jewish and Christian writings, and historical sources. His most recent books are:

- *The Mystery of the Messiah: The Messiahship of Jesus in the Qur'an, New Testament, Old Testament, and Other Sources.*

- *The Mystery of the Crucifixion: The Attempt to Kill Jesus in the Qur'an, the New Testament, and Historical Sources.*

- *The Mystery of Israel in Ancient Egypt: The Exodus in the Qur'an, the Old Testament, Archaeological Finds, and Historical Sources.*

- *The Mystery of the Historical Jesus: The Messiah in the Qur'an, the Bible, and Historical Sources.*

- *The Prophet Joseph in the Qur'an, the Bible, and History: A new detailed commentary on the Qur'anic Chapter of Joseph.*

Surely this Qur'an guides to the way that is straightest and gives good tidings to the believers who do good works that theirs shall be a great reward.

(Qur'an, 17.9)

Contents

Preface 1

Introduction 3

1. The Prophet, the Book, and the Religion 11
    Prophet Muhammad 11
    The Qur'an 14
    Islam...19

2. The Meaning of Jihad 23
    "Jihad" in the Arabic Language..23
    "Jihad" in the Qur'an...24

3. Armed Jihad.. 29
    The Pre-Armed Jihad Period 29
    The Divine Permission for Armed Jihad.......................................31
    A Means to Peace 33
    Prohibiting Aggression and Enjoining Forgiveness....................38
    Measured and Proportionate Retaliation 40
    Warning Against the Abuse of Armed Jihad 42
    The Prohibition of Forcing People into Islam..............................44
    Is Christianity More Peaceful Than Islam?..................................48

4. Peaceful Jihad.. 55
    Peaceful Jihad in Meccan Verses..55
    Aspects of Peaceful Jihad 56
    The War Against the Lower Self 60
    Peaceful Jihad in Prophetic Sayings 61

5. Misreading the Qur'anic Term of "Jihad" 63
    The Erroneous Reduction of Jihad to Armed Jihad 63
    The Distinction Between Jihad and Qitāl (Fighting)...................66

6. Jihad Today 69
    The Essentiality of Jihad..69
    Islamic Retaliation to Aggression..72
    "Islamic" Violence or "Western" Double Standards?..................73
    Muslims in Present Day Conflicts..77
    Qur'anic Peace and the World Today 79

7. The Reality of Jihad... 83

A. The Qur'anic Verses That Contain the Term "Jihad" 87

B. A Brief Chronology of the Life of Prophet Muhammad 93

References 95

Index of Qur'anic Verses 97

Index of Names and Subjects 99

Preface

My wife, Shetha, and I moved from Iraq to the UK in 1992. I quickly came to love so many things about the new culture I was joining. Among other things, democracy, freedom of speech, and human rights are great. They were clearly manifested in the free media. It was a complete contrast to the state-controlled media we left back in our country of origin. There, both the educated and the illiterate knew that what was in the newspapers and on radio and TV is what the dictatorial regime wanted people to believe. People, therefore, sought news and information from foreign media, such as the BBC World Service and Voice of America.

But I soon realized that that the freedom of press in the UK, and the West in general, was at times being mistaken for and equated to accurate reporting if not explicitly then implicitly. It is not that people did not know that the media can, for instance, be manipulative and that while it is not run by the state it is still influenced by powerful individuals and groups. The British in particular have a healthy, natural dose of cynicism in general anyway. But they still relied on that same media for most of the information on what goes on in various parts of the world. Yet I found so much persistent misinformation and misreporting about things I knew very well, either because there were about the country I came from or the Middle East, which I also was very familiar with.

Islam is one aspect of that *other world* that the British and Western media has failed to portray accurately. The religion that I had chosen to embrace in my early twenties in Iraq had developed a very negative image in my new home. Not that this was a complete surprise, but reading about something is one thing and experiencing it is another.

For several years, the idea of writing a book that dispels some of the common misconceptions about Islam was on my mind. I was particularly interested in writing about the unfair and misleading association of Islam with violence and aggression. After the terrorist attacks of the 11th of September 2001 and subsequent sad events, I decided that I should not postpone this project any longer.

The first edition of this book came out in 2002 and a revision was released two years later. In the past five years, so much happened but not much changed, as far as the subject of this book is concerned. Islam is still being singled out for the link to terrorism, those who are keen on this link would not say what terrorism is, and atrocities against Muslims and violence by others are often carefully given different labels. Also, atrocities continue to be committed under the name of jihad. The third edition of the book remains as relevant today as its first edition was seven years earlier.

In the second edition I added more material and improved the readability of the book. In this edition I have also added some new material but I have also removed more content that I do not see as necessary. For instance, the first chapter of the first and second editions discussed in detail how the image of Islam has been distorted by both Muslims and non-Muslims. While I think making references to this fact in certain places in the book remains necessary, I do not find having a complete chapter wholly justified.

By clearly presenting verifiable facts and dispelling unfounded fallacies about jihad I pray that this book can achieve two goals for two different audiences. **First**, it would prove a useful source of information for Muslims and those who will be on their way to Islam.

Second, it would convince non-Muslims that Islam is a peaceful religion that is easy to coexist with. It is a religion under which various religious groups, including Christians and Jews, always lived peacefully and with their religious rights fully protected.

Unfortunately, the gap between Muslims and non-Muslims in the world has been widening. Equally sad is the fact that many do not know that although this conflict involves Muslim believers, it does not owe its origin to the religion of Islam. I, like many others, feel a sense of personal responsibility to help in bridging the growing gap between Muslims and non-Muslims. Such attempts, if done properly, are one form of jihad, as we shall see in this study.

Like all of my other writings, this book has benefited greatly from the insightful and detailed feedback of my wife Dr Shetha Al-Dargazelli. Shetha's support and help have been instrumental in allowing me to write my books.

The comments of my friend Mr Tariq Chaudhry have allowed me to improve the book significantly.

I would like to acknowledge the help of a number of people who reviewed drafts of the earlier editions of the book and provided valuable feedback. I would like to thank my brothers Duraid and Faiz, and my friends Dr Howard Hall, Mr David Barnes, and Mr David Mercer. I would also like to thank all readers and reviewers whose feedback made me write and improve this new edition.

Introduction

There has been much disagreement and differing views about what Islam really teaches. This debate has not raged between Muslims and non-Muslims only, but different Muslim groups have also adopted contradictory views, so no wonder that non-Muslims do not share one common understanding. Jihad is one of those hotly contested Islamic concepts, having generated so much disagreement and diametrically opposed interpretations. In the Western media, jihad is often used in Islamophobic contexts where it is presented as denoting the *killing of innocent people, often non-Muslims, by militant Muslims* for a political cause. An additional slant occasionally put on this definition makes this killing the fate of those who resist being forced into embracing Islam. Yet many Muslims argue, as this book does, that jihad is a concept about spiritual development that has no more to do with violence than, say, nationalism or democracy. These have also been abused to justify committing all kinds of violence, including starting devastating wars. There are a number of causes for the development of such contrasting views of jihad.

First, although the Qur'an is the only sacred book of Islam, it is not the only source used to derive Islamic teachings from. The other main source is the compilations of sayings and doings attributed to the Prophet Muhammad, known as "hadith." These reports — which are also referred to as "sunnah," which means "way of life" — were first recorded almost 100 years after the Prophet and contain inconsistent and even contradictory accounts. Different Muslim groups disagree about which compilations are more authentic, with the two biggest branches of Islam, Sunnism and Shiasm, adopting different sources of hadith.

But even scholars within any one school of thought or denomination differ on the authenticity of various alleged Prophetic sayings and doings! Yet all agree that many sayings and actions attributed to the Prophet have been fabricated by various people over time for a variety of purposes. Nevertheless, hadith has been extensively used for interpreting and extrapolating the Qur'an and as the second source of legislation in Islam. For instance, punishment by stoning is not mentioned in the Qur'an, but its adherents argue that its reports in hadith establish its legitimacy. Similarly, the Qur'anic concept of jihad has been understood in various ways by different groups and individuals partly due to their influence by hadith.

This is why I focus in this book on studying the concept of jihad in the Qur'an. The Qur'an is the undisputed source of Islam and authority on all of its aspects. With its exclusive emphasis on the Qur'an, this book sets itself apart from other studies of jihad which, at best, mix with the Qur'an secondary religious and historical sources or, at worst, focus on them. I have quoted a few Prophetic sayings that are in line with Qur'anic verses I discuss. But I have consciously avoided using Prophetic sayings or any other sources to reach conclusions that the Qur'an does not explicitly support. Using only the Qur'an reveals a picture of jihad that is very different from its common image.

This source of misunderstanding jihad has claimed both Muslim and non-Muslim victims.

Second, in some Muslim countries and communities, the elite of religious leaders have adopted misguided views of Islamic concepts such as jihad. The potentially devastating influence of these twisted views is then realized by uninformed, often poorly educated, followers. These followers are separated from the reality of their religion by the scantiness of their knowledge of Islam — something that is sustained by their passive surrender to their misleading leaders. Their understanding of, say, jihad, is whatever they are taught by those leaders. This poor leadership is, at times, the result of genuine ignorance and poor understanding of Islam and, at others, the consequence of deliberate manipulation of Islamic teachings for power and personal gains.

There is a substantial difference between the effects of the ignorance of the average Muslim and the person who takes a pseudo educational and/or leading role in society. The latter creates a much wider audience, possibly of non-Muslims as well as Muslims, for his distorted version of Islamic teachings. This problem is made worse by the fact that so many Muslims inherit and accept a passive attitude toward self-education, relying uncritically and almost entirely on the teachings of whatever past or contemporary clerics or scholars they happen to know or learn about. Like any student, the seeker of knowledge needs teachers, but it is equally important that these teachers are genuine. The Qur'an enjoins on the Muslim seeking knowledge proactively. This involves more than total and uncritical reliance on the opinions of a couple of scholars. All of this is best illustrated in this Prophetic saying:

> He who initiates a good practice will earn a reward for that and a reward equal to the rewards of those who follow it, without the latter's rewards reducing. He who initiates a bad practice will earn a sin for that and a sin equal to the sins of those who follow it, without the latter's sins reducing. (*Musnad Ahmad*, saying 19719)

This tradition emphasizes the big responsibility of the teachers and the effect that they can have on society. At the same time, it does not take away the responsibility from those who follow pseudo teachers. A genuine learner would carefully scrutinize any claim made by a book, teacher, or any source of information. Commitment to seeking knowledge is an intrinsic part of Islam, and one aspect of this commitment is the careful examination of the available sources of information.

This source of misinformation about jihad has influenced mainly susceptible Muslims who follow such false leaders. But the West has also treated such leaders as legitimate presenters of jihad. Western media could have been a lot better informed about Islam and fairer in presenting it, but it has not been more culpable than those ignorant Muslims that it uses as sources of information on Islam.

Third, from its early days, Islam was subjected to *deliberate* distortion by followers of competing religions, mainly Christianity and Judaism. This propaganda continued down the centuries, although religion became only one of its drivers. Political and economic interests as well as a sense of cultural superiority have maintained those myths about Islam and make them deep-rooted in the Western mind. This is what the author of *Western Views of Islam in the Middle Ages* says:

> There can be little doubt that at the moment of their formation these legends and fantasies were taken to represent a more or less truthful account of what they purported to describe. But as soon as they were produced they took on a literary life of their own. At the level of popular poetry, the picture of Mahomet and his Saracens changed very little from generation to generation. Like well-loved characters of fiction, they were expected to display certain characteristics, and authors faithfully reproduced them for hundreds of years. (Southern, 1978: 29)

Some Western commentators have tried to ignore this centuries-long trend of misinformation to try and suggest that the issues *the world*, by which they mean *the Western world*, currently has with Islam and Muslims are issues of today. Acknowledging that hostility to Islam has always occupied some space in the Western psyche would not produce an interesting and simplistic enough theory that explains international conflicts for those who prefer simplicity to accuracy and truth. For instance, in an article expressively titled *The Age of Muslim Wars*, professor Samuel Huntington, advocate of the controversial "Clash of Civilizations" theory, made the following sweeping statement:

> Contemporary global politics is the age of Muslim wars. Muslims fight each other and fight non-Muslims far more often than do peoples of other civilizations. Muslim wars have replaced the cold war as the principal form of

international conflict. These wars include wars of terrorism, guerrilla wars, civil wars and interstate conflicts. These instances of Muslim violence could congeal into one major clash of civilizations between Islam and the West or between Islam and the Rest.

Throughout history, the West continued to see Islam in negative images that reflected what was considered to be bad and evil at the time. Myths about Islam took different forms in different periods in history. The inferiority of Islam was always considered a fact, though its supposed proof changed with time. Karen Armstrong (2001: 43) cites a couple of modern stereotypical images of Islam:

> We constantly produce new prototypes to express our apparently ingrained hatred of "Islam." In the 1970s we were haunted by the image of the immensely rich oil sheikh; in the 1980s by the fanatical ayatollah; since the Salman Rushdie affair, "Islam" has become a religion that spells death to creativity and artistic freedom. But none of these images reflects the reality, which is infinitely more complex. Yet this does not stop people from making sweeping and inaccurate judgements.

Clearly, this source of distortion of jihad has affected non-Muslims.

Four, while it can be seen as one form of the third cause, I would list "double standards" as a separate source for the distorted image that the West has successfully cultivated and maintained of Islam. Treating Islam and Muslims one way and others in a different way contributed to the development of the misunderstanding of jihad among Muslims and non-Muslims alike. It prevented the latter from taking an objective view about jihad, but it also alienated many Muslims, driving some of them to extremism and ultimately terrorism in which they use the concept of jihad to justify their atrocities. The decades-long devastating injustice that the Palestinians have endured as a result of Israeli aggression, which has received full support from the West, has been the source of a considerable amount of suffering and unrest for the whole world. Many terrorists have been driven to committing atrocities as a result of seeing this kind of injustice being inflicted for years on millions of people they identified with.

One common form of double standards is to link evil committed by Muslims to Islam but not do the same in the case of other groups and beliefs. Ancient and modern history provides so many examples of national, political, and religious leaders, representing various political persuasions and religious faiths, inciting violence against their opponents and those who did not share their beliefs. Yet not all those political philosophies and religions get tarnished because of what individuals who believed in them did or said. Christianity is one case in point. The massacre of many thousands of Muslims at the hands of Christians in places such as Serbia, Kosovo, and Chechnya did not earn the religion of those who committed atrocities any association with terrorism. Of course, any such connection would have been wrong and unfair, but the same logic should be applied in the case of Muslims who commit evil acts. Alas, it is double standards in its ugly display.

Those double standards are also behind the insistence of those who supposedly oppose "terrorism" on using this term without defining it! Defining terrorism would expose those who would like to use the term conveniently, showing them at least as terrorist sympathizers but at times as terrorists themselves.

Take "suicide bombing" as another example. Suicide bombers often indiscriminately kill innocent people, and it is right to condemn such atrocities. But is it really worse than, say, cluster bombs? Israel has used the latter regularly, killing many more than suicide bombing has done. Yet the use of cluster bombs does not evoke as much negative image, abhorrence, and condemnation. What about the use of depleted uranium against Iraq and its devastating effect on the population? But even traditional weapons can be worse than suicide bombing. And what about raining tons of traditional bombs, as the USA, Israel, and their allies do in their wars? Why would this not be seen as appalling and criminal as "suicide bombing"? The reason is the same that lies behind not defining "terrorism." Self-righteousness and self-interests are the main drivers for these and all forms of double standards.

These are the four main causes for the very different views of the reality of jihad.

The objective of this book is to explain the concept of jihad according to the Qur'an. Naturally, the book quotes extensively from the Qur'an. In some places it may even read like a commentary on Qur'anic verses.

Because of the nature and structure of the Qur'an, which I discuss in Chapter 1, the relevant verses about jihad are found throughout the Qur'an. By collating all those verses and looking at them together, it is possible to see in those verses common themes and complementary meanings that might not be visible when the verses are studied separately.

I have tried my best to make this book self-contained, requiring no knowledge of the Qur'an or Islamic history and thought. All necessary information and explanations are given where needed to make this focused study an easy read.

Here is a brief look at the book's seven chapters and two appendices.

Chapter 1 provides necessary background information for the investigation of the concept of jihad. It first gives a brief biography of

Prophet Muhammad. Next, it introduces the Qur'an — the book that was revealed to the Prophet and is the sacred book of the religion of Islam. The chapter concludes by explaining Islam. This term denotes the one religion that God revealed to all the prophets He sent.

In **Chapter 2**, the general meaning of the Arabic word jihad is first examined. This term refers to exerting efforts, involving some form of "struggle" and "resistance," to achieve a particular goal. Qur'anic jihad is a special case of jihad where the efforts are exerted in practicing Islam. Qur'anic Jihad can be divided into "armed jihad" and "peaceful jihad." The former, temporary form of jihad refers to the Muslims' reaction to armed aggression. Peaceful jihad is mainly the Muslim's permanent struggle against the evil desires within the self. It also covers the peaceful struggle against any form of evil in the world. The common belief that jihad means "holy war" is wrong and misleading. This misunderstanding reflects the failure to notice, among other things, that the Qur'an uses mainly the term "qitāl" when talking about fighting an enemy. This Arabic word means "fighting."

Armed jihad is examined in **Chapter 3**. It was fourteen years after the revelation of the Qur'an before God granted the Muslims permission to fight back aggression and defend themselves. The ultimate aim of armed jihad is peace. God has attached many strings to His permission to the Muslims to resort to arms in response to violent aggression. Muslims are prohibited from committing aggression. Their response must be measured and proportionate. Armed jihad must not be used for any purpose other than self-defense. It is not, for instance, for forcing people into Islam.

Chapter 4 studies peaceful jihad. While it covers the peaceful struggle against any source of evil, the main form of peaceful jihad is the person's struggle against the inferior drives of his lower self. This kind of jihad is essential for spiritual development, so the Muslim must never abandon it. Various aspects of the struggle against the lower self are examined in this chapter.

Reducing jihad to its armed form only, thus ignoring peaceful jihad, involves misreading references to jihad in some verses as meaning armed jihad when they actually mean jihad in general, both armed and peaceful. This is explained in **Chapter 5**. Another cause for this misunderstanding is confusing the terms "jihad" and "qitāl."

After examining various aspects of jihad in the Qur'an in the previous chapters, jihad in today's world is investigated in **Chapter 6**. Peaceful jihad is as essential a practice for the Muslim today as it was in the past. The Muslim, in fact, must live in a permanent state of struggle against his/her lower self.

The way armed jihad is being applied reflects much misunderstanding of this form of jihad and ignorance of the rules that govern fighting in Islam. The concept of jihad has been misused and abused by various Muslim individuals and groups. Some have portrayed it as the means to establish an Islamic state. Others have used it to justify their or other Muslims' vengeful responses to aggression. The term jihad is also often used today by various Muslim groups to describe their role in any armed struggles. Many have failed to understand that armed jihad applies only in particular circumstances.

Misunderstanding today's world can only worsen the consequences of that mix of misunderstanding and ignorance. The double standards of the West, its tolerance of the suffering of Muslims in various parts of the world, and its involvement at times in injustices against Muslims have contributed directly to the abuse of the concept of jihad by some under the name of Islam.

The Qur'an promotes and calls for peace. Muslims need to put more efforts in establishing peace. They can achieve with peace more than they can do using any other means.

In addition to the ongoing struggle against the lower self, one other major form of jihad today is the struggle to remove all misconceptions about Islam and educate people about this great religion. This is as important a duty on every Muslim as any of the fundamentals of Islam.

Chapter 7 summarizes the conclusions drawn throughout the book and reaffirms the reality of jihad.

The book has two appendices. **Appendix A** lists all Qur'anic verses that contain any variation of the term jihad. A short chronology of the life of Prophet Muhammad is given in **Appendix B**.

For easy reference, the book includes an index of all of Qur'anic verses quoted or cited in the book and another index of names and subjects.

The book uses a number of styles. Each Qur'anic verse has been followed by a combination of two numbers identifying its *sūra* or "chapter" and its position in that chapter. For instance, the combination 4.172 refers to chapter 4, verse 172.

Although I have consulted some English translations of the Qur'an, the translations in this book are mine. I always use my own translations of the Qur'an as translation is an act of interpretation, reflecting the translator's understanding of the text. For Biblical quotes, I have used the *King James Version*.

Square brackets have been used to enclose explanatory texts that are needed to clarify the translation. Alternative texts, such as the English meaning of a term that is quoted in its Arabic origin, are enclosed in parentheses.

The book uses a number of different printing styles. Different fonts have been used for the main text, Qur'anic verses, and Biblical passages. Roman transliterations of Arabic terms are in italics.

Finally, I welcome any feedback from readers at the following email address   fatoohi.public.1@gmail.com   or   through   my   website www.quranicstudies.com.

1

The Prophet, the Book, and the Religion

Before studying jihad in the Qur'an, we need to look briefly at the historical context in which the Qur'an was revealed and how it was received by people. This aspect of the early history of Islam helps understand jihad, and indeed many other concepts in the Qur'an. It is ultimately helpful to understand Islam properly.

Prophet Muhammad

Prophet Muhammad was born in 570 CE in the city of Mecca in the Arabian Peninsula, part of modern day Saudi Arabia. His father died before he was born, so his paternal grandfather, 'Abd al-Muṭṭalib, became his guardian.

'Abd al-Muṭṭalib was the respected head of the clan of Hāshim and the tribe of Quraysh, to which his clan belonged. With the Quraysh being the biggest and most influential tribe in Mecca, 'Abd al-Muṭṭalib was seen as the master of all of Mecca. The Quraysh had a special status in Mecca because they were in charge of the sacred Kaʻba. The Qur'an tells us that this holy edifice was built by prophets Abraham and his son Ishmael:

> When Abraham and Ishmael were raising the foundations of the House [Abraham prayed]: "Our Lord! Accept from us [our works]. Surely, You are the Hearing, the Knowing. (2.127) Our Lord! Make us Muslims and raise from our offspring a nation of Muslims. Show us our ways of worship, and relent toward us. Surely, Your are the Relenting, the Merciful." (2.128)

This dates the building of the Kaʻba to around 1900 BCE, which is when Abraham is thought to have lived. The Kaʻba maintained down the centuries its venerable status as the destination of pilgrimage for the Arab population of the Arabian Peninsula, although Abraham's original religion was forgotten over time and people developed pagan beliefs. 'Abd al-Muṭṭalib was personally in charge of the Kaʻba.

The Prophet was only five to six years old when he lost his mother. Two years later, the little orphan lost his grandfather and custodian 'Abd al-Muṭṭalib. Now one of 'Abd al-Muṭṭalib's sons, Abū Ṭālib, became the guardian of his orphan nephew. Though respected by the clan of Hāshim and the people of Mecca in general, Abū Ṭālib did not have the high status and influence of his father. Had he been more fortunate financially, he might have aspired to acquire that special position of leadership.

When Muhammad was twenty five years old, he was hired by a wealthy Meccan lady called Khadīja to sell her merchandize in Syria. Khadīja, a widow fifteen years Muhammad's senior, later proposed marriage to him, which he agreed to. They lived together for almost a quarter of a century, but Khadīja died about 8-9 years after the revelation of the Qur'an.

Muhammad did not get married to another woman during Khadīja's life, despite the fact that polygyny was common practice in that society. Living out his youth with only one woman in that highly polygynous environment contradicts Muhammad's lecherous image in the Western mind.

Muhammad was deeply interested in spiritual matters. His oldest surviving biography by Ibn Hisham (died 833 CE), which is a freely edited version of Ibn Ishaq's (ca. 704 - 767 CE), tells us that before the revelation of the Qur'an Muhammad used to retreat for a month every year in a cave. After finishing his seclusion he would return to circumbulate the Ka'ba seven times before heading home.

The cave itself, which survived the times, gives a very vivid image of Muhammad's spiritual inclinations. Resting on the top of one of the mountains north of Mecca, Hira', the cave is completely isolated from the rest of the world. In my first visit to the mountain and after arriving to the summit and knowing that I was very close to the cave, I still failed to know how to find the cave and had to be guided to by other visitors who had seen it before!

But how could Muhammad have known about this well hidden cave? Muhammad must have been divinely guided to that hideaway, even if he had chosen to climb the mountain consciously.

The top of Hira' is surely one of the loneliest places in that mountainous desert of Mecca. But the cave, and also the small courtyard in front of it, is even more isolated. If you stand up in the courtyard, you can only look over the surrounding rocks at the desert or, these days, buildings that are hundreds of meters down and several kilometers away. If you sit down, the surrounding rocks are just too high for you to see anything other than the sky. Inside the cave you are completely surrounded by the rocky walls. It is total isolation and complete emptiness. There is nothing of this world there to see or get distracted by — an ideal place for someone who wanted to forget the world and focus on what lies beyond the present, visible, and material. The inhabitant of that cave was obviously interested in things beyond this world and its material riches. I have described the cave in more detail with photos taken by me in an article on my website (Fatoohi, 2007a).

It was in that cave in 610 CE, i.e. at the age of forty, during the month of Ramadhan that Muhammad was visited by the angel Gabriel who read to him the first verses of the Qur'an. This is how the mountain of Ḥira' became known as the mountain of "*Nūr* (light)". The Qur'an continued to be revealed in fragments to Prophet Muhammad over the following twenty two years. The last words of the Book were revealed to the Prophet shortly before his death in 632 CE (p. 15).

In the first three years after the revelation, the Prophet preached Islam secretly to individuals he trusted. The number of converts in this period is estimated to have been no more than forty. It is believed that the divine command to the Prophet to go public came in this verse: "Therefore, declare publicly what you are commanded and turn away from the polytheists" (15.94). When he went public with his call to Islam, the new religion started gradually to attract more people. Not surprisingly, the hostility of the idol worshipping population of Mecca also grew. The Prophet was subjected to harassment and abuse. Armed with patience, resilience, and determination, and protected by his uncle Abū Ṭālib and the clan of Hāshim, the Prophet was able to carry on preaching the new faith.

Converts to Islam, some of whom were slaves, had to suffer at the hands of the enemies of the new religion all forms of persecution, including brutal torture and murder. In 614 CE, the Prophet instructed a group of Muslims to escape the persecution to Abyssinia and seek the protection of its just Christian king. The Quraysh sent a delegation to the king, carrying precious gifts, to secure the extradition of the Muslim refugees. But appreciating the similarities between the new religion and Christianity and touched by the venerated position of Jesus in the Qur'an, the king rejected the bribe and let the Muslims stay in Abyssinia.

One year later, the Quraysh imposed economic and social sanctions on the Prophet, his followers, and his clan. As a result, the Muslims withdrew to a mountain in Mecca. The sanctions lasted for about three years before collapsing in 618/619 CE without achieving their goals.

Soon afterward, the Prophet lost his wife Khadīja. Matters got worse quickly with the death of his uncle and protector. Prophet Muhammad started to suffer more from the disbelievers as they continued their attempts to uproot Islam and destroy its followers. During the pilgrimage season in 622 CE, Muhammad met in Mecca with a number of chiefs from the city of Yathrib, where he had previously sent some Muslims to settle in. Having converted to Islam, the chiefs made a secret pledge to protect the Prophet should the Quraysh try to kill him.

The Quraysh learned about the agreement, so the people from Yathrib had to return quickly to their city. Sensing that the danger to Muslims has increased, Muhammad instructed them to immigrate individually and in small groups to Yathrib. The Qurayshites tried to prevent Muslims from fleeing Mecca, but the converts continued to sneak out of the city.

The continuing immigration of Muslims to Yathrib where they had allies was already bad enough news for the Qurayshites. Things could get even much worse if Muhammad also would move to that city. They decided that they had no option but to kill him.

The various clans of the tribe of Quraysh agreed to act as one and assassinate the Prophet in his sleep. Acting collectively would mean that no one party could be blamed for the murder and become embroiled in a war of vengeance with the clan of Hāshim.

The assassination plan, however, was sabotaged by divine intervention. The night the murder was planned to take place, God informed His Prophet of the danger and ordered him to secretly leave Mecca and head to Yathrib, about 350 kilometers north of Mecca. The latter became known as "al-Madīna al-Munawwara (the illuminated city)", or "Medina" in English, after the arrival of the Prophet.

This famous event, known as the "*Hijra* (immigration)", occurred in 622 CE, about twelve years after the revelation of the first verses of the Qur'an. This flight was destined to have far-reaching consequences in establishing Islam and growing and protecting its followers. The Prophet lived in Medina for about ten years. By the time of his departure from this world in 632 CE, Islam had become well established as the religion of the Arabian Peninsula and had made inroads in neighboring regions. Muslims had become a major force to be reckoned with in the area.

For easy reference, Appendix B contains a short chronology of major events in the life of Prophet Muhammad. There are a number of detailed English biographies of Prophet Muhammad. One biography written by a non-Muslim is Karen Armstrong's *Muhammad: A Biography of the Prophet*. Another one written by a Muslim is Martin Lings' *Muhammad: His Life Based on the Earliest Sources*.

The Qur'an

The Qur'an is a continuation of the previous divine Messages that God sent to people via His messengers throughout history. It is the grand finale of those divine messages. To the polytheistic Arabs of Mecca, nevertheless, Islam was a new religion. We will look in more detail at the message of the Qur'an in the next section.

The Qur'an consists of 114 chapters, and each chapter (*sūra* in Arabic) consists of a number of verses (*āyāt*). The longest chapter, which is number 2, contains 286 verses, whereas chapters 103, 108, and 110 consist of only 3 verses each. The Qur'an contains 6236 verses in total.

Out of the 114 chapters, 86 were revealed over twelve years when the Prophet was still living in Mecca . The other 28 chapters were revealed in Medina. These Medinite chapters include some of the longest chapters of the Qur'an. This is why although they represent about 25% of the Qur'anic chapters, the Medinite chapters make up about 40% of the Qur'an. A number of the latter Medinite chapters contain detailed information on legal issues and answer various questions that continued to come up as a Muslim community was emerging.

The overwhelming majority of scholars consider the following verses to be the first that were revealed to the Prophet:

Read [O Muhammad!] in the name of your Lord who created. (96.1) He created man from a clot. (96.2) Read, and your Lord is the Most Honorable (96.3) who taught with the pen (96.4) — taught man what he knew not. (96.5)

Scholars are in far less agreement on which verse was revealed last. This verse is considered as one likely candidate:

Guard yourselves against a day in which you shall be returned to Allah; then every soul shall be paid back in full what it has earned, and they (the souls) will not be wronged. (2.281)

Note that the verses that were revealed first belong to chapter number 96 rather than 1. Similarly, the last verse that the Prophet received is not from chapter number 114. The reason is that chapters are not compiled in the Qur'an in the chronological order of their revelation. Chapter 1 in the compiled Qur'an is not the chapter that was revealed first and chapter 114 was not last.

Additionally, it is not uncommon to find that the verses within a chapter are not all arranged in the chronological order of their revelation. For instance, several Meccan chapters contain some Medinite verses also.

These particular arrangements of the chapters and of the verses within each chapter in the compiled Qur'an are considered to be a genuine part of the structure of the Qur'an. In other words, the verses and the chapters were arranged in this way by Prophet Muhammad as he was taught by God.

The verses of any one chapter, apart from shorter chapters, usually address a number of different issues. Accordingly, successive verses do not necessarily talk about the same subject.

Those who are familiar with the style of the Bible get surprised, and even baffled, when they read a translation of the Qur'an. Unlike the Bible, the Qur'an is not a history book. Although it contains historical stories about past, good and evil individuals and nations, it has a unique style even in relating history. The Qur'an is not interested in pure history. Historical accounts are mentioned in order to highlight their didactic lessons. For instance, the Qur'an often bypasses details that are given prominence in traditional recounting of history. To mention one example, it is common for the Qur'an not to name main characters and places in a story. Examples of prominent characters in Qur'anic stories whose names are not mentioned include Adam's wife and two sons and Joseph's eleven brothers. For more information about the style of the Qur'an, the reader may consult *History in the Qur'an* in my book *The Mystery of the Historical Jesus.*

The Qur'an's unique style reflects the fact that it is the *literal words of God* to His Messenger Muhammad. Note for instance this verse:

> They (the believers) ask you [O Muhammad!] as to how they should spend [for charity]. Say: "Whatever wealth you spend, it is for the parents, the near of kin, the orphans, the needy, and the wayfarer. Whatever good you do, Allah surely knows it." (2.215)

Rather than containing only instructions from God on how people should spend their money for charity, this verse is an *exact* copy of the words that God revealed to Muhammad in this respect. The words were not edited by the Prophet to include only the ultimate message that God wanted to reach people, but he delivered them in their entirety and exactly as he received them.

There are also verses that addressed personal matters of the Prophet, although of course they convey useful lessons to people in general. For example, this short chapter which was revealed to the Prophet at a difficult time reminded him of God's favors to him and gave him support and patience:

> I swear by the early hours of the day (93.1) and the night when it covers with darkness (93.2) that your Lord has not forsaken you, nor has He become displeased [with you]. (93.3) Surely, the hereafter is better for you than the first life. (93.4) Your Lord will give you so that you shall be well pleased. (93.5) Did He not find you an orphan and give you shelter, (93.6) did He not find you wandering and guide you, (93.7) and did He not find you in need and make you independent? (93.8) Therefore, as for the orphan, do not oppress him; (93.9) as for the beggar, do not chide him; (93.10) and as for the favor of your Lord, do speak about it. (93.11)

The Qur'an was revealed in an environment that produced poets who had impressive mastery of Arabic and authored magnificent poetry. The

Arabs were fond of poetry and honored it to the extent that they hung seven particularly impressive poems on the walls of the sacred Ka'ba. They also used poetry to ridicule their enemies and glorify their tribes. A war between two tribes that lasts a few hours or a day may be followed by a war of words that could last for years. Winning or losing this less bloody war was seen almost equally significant.

Even those Arabs were completely overwhelmed and intrigued by the majestic power and beauty of the language of the Qur'an. It was in their language, but it showed unprecedented mastery of Arabic that filled them with awe. The Qur'an has always been seen as an unparalleled piece of Arabic. It can only be described as a linguistic miracle. The Qur'an itself challenged the Arabs who questioned its divine origin to produce any text of similar quality:

> This Qur'an is not such that it could be forged by those besides Allah, but it is a confirmation of the Book that was revealed before it and an exposition of It — there is no doubt about that — from the Lord of the peoples. (10.37) Or do they (the disbelievers) say: "He (Muhammad) has forged it"? Say [O Muhammad!]: "Then come up with a chapter like it and call [for help] whom you can besides Allah, if you were truthful." (10.38)

> If you [O People!] are in doubt as to that which We have revealed to Our servant [Muhammad], then come up with a chapter like it and call [for help] your witnesses besides Allah, if you were truthful. (2.23) But if you do not do it, and surely you shall never do it, then guard yourselves against the Fire whose fuel is people and stones; it is prepared for the disbelievers. (2.24)

One aspect of the uniqueness of the Qur'anic text, which was written down at the time of its revelation, is that it did not change over time. This is the view of the overwhelming majority of scholars, both Muslim and non-Muslim. The Qur'an itself proclaims that it is protected by God against any attempt to tamper with it:

> Verily, it is We who revealed the Remembrance (the Qur'an), and verily We are its Guardian. (15.9)

Another verse stresses that the Qur'an will remain protected against any form of falsehood at all time:

> Surely, those who disbelieved in the Remembrance (the Qur'an) when it came to them [were wrong]. Surely, it is an impregnable Book. (41.41) Falsehood cannot come to it from anywhere; [it is] a revelation from One who is Wise and Praised. (41.42)

Simply put, the Qur'an that we read today is the same Book that was revealed to Prophet Muhammad about 14 centuries ago. This is in contrast to the Jewish and Christian scriptures. The Qur'an states in several verses that people tampered with divine Books that God revealed to previous Prophets:

> Woe, then, to those who write the book with their hands and then say "This is from Allah" to get a small price for it; therefore, woe to them for what their hands have written, and woe to them for what they earn. (2.79)

This 14-century old verdict is shared today by the overwhelming majority of scholars of the Old and New Testaments who agree that the versions of these books that we have today are the product of editorial processes that happened over centuries and involved many people.

The Qur'an states that Allah revealed to Moses a Book called the "Tawrāt (Torah)" and to Jesus a Book called the "Injīl." Other Prophets who were given Scriptures include Abraham and David. While slightly influenced by such divine Books, the surviving Jewish and Christian scriptures have been mainly written and edited by man.

This unique attribute of the Qur'an doesn't apply to any other Islamic religious text. Even the highly regarded compilations of sayings of Prophet Muhammad contain many entries whose authenticity has always been the subject of disagreement among scholars. Although several different doctrines have evolved within Islam, the authenticity of the Qur'an is universally accepted.

I would like to quickly mention the accusation that the Qur'an is based on the Old and New Testaments. This accusation has been popular since the West became aware of the Qur'an (e.g. Tisdall, 1905). The Qur'an has similarities with Jewish and Christian sources, but it has substantially more differences. The similarities are actually almost negligible when compared with the differences. Furthermore, when differing accounts of the Qur'an and Jewish and Christian sources of an event are checked against independent sources, the Qur'anic version of events proves to be the more accurate.

To explain such similarities and differences from the Qur'anic perspective, I coined in an earlier book the term "contextual displacement." This term denotes a special kind of "textual corruption" in Jewish and Christian writings where "a character, event, or statement appears in one context in the Qur'an and in a different context in other sources." Contextual displacements are the result of "the Bible's editors moving figures, events, and statements from their correct, original contexts" (Fatoohi, 2007b: 39). I have discussed in detail in a number of my works many instances where the authors of the Bible and other Jewish and Christian sources placed events in wrong contexts (Fatoohi 2007b, 2007c, 2008, 2009; Fatoohi & Al-Dargazelli, 2008).

Islam

A common misconception about Islam is that it is the religion that was revealed to Prophet Muhammad only. Islam, the Qur'an tells us, is rather the name of the one religion that Allah, the one and only God, revealed to every Prophet that He sent to people since the time of the first man and Prophet, Adam. For instance, all the following Prophets were Muslims who practiced and taught Islam: Noah, Abraham, Ishmael, Isaac, Jacob, Joseph, Moses, Aaron, David, Solomon, Zachariah, John, and Jesus. The following verse describes Israelite Prophets as "Muslims":

> Surely, We revealed the Torah in which there was guidance and light; with it, the prophets who *aslamū* (became Muslims) guided the Jews. (from 5.44)

There is a major difference between the use of the term "prophet" in the Qur'an and the Bible. Prophethood in the Qur'an denotes a special, elevated status in which a man receives revelation from God and acts as His messenger to teach people the true religion. Biblical prophethood, on the other hand, is associated with prophecies, though facilitated by God.

The name "Muslim" was coined by God who used it long before the time of Prophet Muhammad and the Qur'an, as revealed in the following verse:

> *Jāhidū* (do jihad) [O you who believe!] in the way of Allah *jihādihi* (the kind of jihad that is due to Him). He has chosen you and has not laid upon you a hardship in religion; it is the faith of your father Abraham. He [Allah] has named you *al-Muslimīn* (the Muslims) earlier and in this (the Qur'an), so that the Messenger be a witness over you, and you be witnesses over people. Therefore keep up prayer, pay the obligatory alms, and hold fast to Allah. He is your Master; so how excellent a Master and how excellent a Supporter! (22.78)

The verse clearly states that God has named the followers of His religion "Muslims" not only in the Qur'an but also in Books that He had revealed to previous prophets, such as the Torah of Moses and the Injīl of Jesus. The following verse states that prophet Noah, who lived long before prophet Abraham, told his people that God ordered him to be "one of the Muslims":

> But if you [O people!] turn away [from my call], I have not asked you for any reward; my reward is only with Allah, and I have been commanded to be one of *al-Muslimīn* (the Muslims). (10.72)

Previous divine Books and prophets used terms equivalent to "Islam" and "Muslim" in their respective languages.

The Arabic verb "*yuslim*" means "surrenders" or "submits." It is used in a special way in the Qur'an to mean "surrenders one's self to God," "submits to God," and so on. The derived Qur'anic noun "*Islām*," therefore, means "submission to God." To be a Muslim is to believe in Allah as the one Lord, submit to His will, and carry out His commandments. So, Islam is a universal term that describes the one religion that God instructed, through His various Messengers, all people to embrace. Let's read some of the relevant Qur'anic verses, starting with these about prophets Abraham and his sons and grandsons:

> Who has a better religion than he who *aslama* (has become a Muslim / has surrendered himself) to Allah, is a doer of good, and has followed the faith of Abraham, worshipping one God. Allah took Abraham as a close friend. (4.125)

> Who turns away from the religion of Abraham but he who makes himself a fool. Surely, We chose him (Abraham) in this world, and in the hereafter he is surely among the righteous. (2.130) When his Lord said to him; "*Aslim* (Be a Muslim / submit)," he said: "*Aslamtu* (I have become a Muslim / I have submitted) to the Lord of the peoples." (2.131) And Abraham enjoined the same on his sons, and so did Jacob: "O my sons! Surely, Allah has chosen for you the [true] religion, therefore die not except as *Muslimūn* (Muslims)". (2.132) Or were you [O People of the Book!] witnesses when death visited Jacob, when he said to his sons: "What will you worship after me?"? They said: "We shall worship your God and the God of your fathers, Abraham, Ishmael and Isaac — one God, and to Him we are *Muslimūn* (Muslims)". (2.133)

The following verses about the Jews and Christians, or the "People of the Book," emphasize and command the Prophet to stress that "Islam" or "submission to God" is *the* true religion of the Lord:

> They (the Jews and Christians) say: "No one shall enter Paradise except he who is a Jew or a Christian." These are nothing more than their desires. Say [O Muhammad!]: "Bring your proof if you are truthful." (2.111) Verily, whoever *aslama* (becomes a Muslim / Submits) to Allah and is a doer of good, his reward is with his Lord, and there is no fear for them nor shall they grieve. (2.112)

> Surely, the [true] religion in the sight of Allah is *al-Islām* (Islam), and those to whom the Book had been given differed only after knowledge had come to them, out of transgression among themselves. Whoever denies the verses of Allah, then surely Allah is quick in reckoning. (3.19) But if they argue with you [O Muhammad!], say: "*Aslamtu* (I have become a Muslim / I have surrendered) to Allah and so has everyone who follows me." And say to those who have been given the Book and to the unlearned people: "*A'aslamtum* (Would you become Muslims / would you submit)?" So if *Aslamū* (they become Muslims / they submit) then they have found the right way, but if they turn away, then your responsibility is only the deliverance of the Message; and Allah sees the servants. (3.20)

This verse is about prophet Solomon and the Queen of Sheba who came to visit him in his palace:

It was said to her: "Enter the hall." But when she saw it she deemed it to be a lake of water and bared her legs. He said: "It is a hall made smooth with glass." She said [praying to Allah]: "My Lord! Surely, I have wronged myself, and *aslamtu* (I have become a Muslim / I submit) with Solomon to Allah, the Lord of the peoples." (27.44)

Prophet Muhammad is the last prophet of Islam, and the Qur'an is the last Book from God:

[O people!] Muhammad is not the father of any of your men, but he is the Messenger of Allah and the last of the prophets; and Allah is aware of everything. (33.40)

The Qur'an stresses that, contrary to the claims of the disbelieving Arabs, making a human being a messenger, as happened to Prophet Muhammad, was not an unprecedented event. In fact, this is exactly how God communicated with people: through messengers that carried His message to people:

Say [O Muhammad!]: "I am not the first of the messengers, and I do not know what will be done with me or with you. I only follow that which is revealed to me, and I am only a manifest warner." (46.9)

In addition to the belief in the oneness of God, the hereafter, and the angels, the Qur'an requires the Muslim to believe in all previous messengers and the Books and messages that God revealed to them. This is consistent with the Qur'an's affirmation that all messengers preached the same religion and were sent by the same God. The Muslim is commanded to hold all prophets in high esteem and reverence. The failure to believe in any prophet is a failure to believe in all prophets, and a failure to be a Muslim:

Say [O you who believe!]: "We believe in Allah, in that which has been revealed to us; in that which was revealed to Abraham, Ishmael, Isaac, Jacob, and the Descendents (Jacob's sons); in that which was given to Moses and Jesus; and in that which was given to the prophets from their Lord. We do not discriminate between any of them, and to Him we are *Muslimūn* (Muslims)". (2.136)

The Messenger (Muhammad) believes in that which has been revealed to him from his Lord, and so do the believers. They all believe in Allah, His angels, His Books, and His messengers. [They say] "we make no distinction between any of His messengers"; and they say: "We hear and obey [Allah's commandments]; grant us Your forgiveness, our Lord. To You is the eventual course." (2.285)

Islam is not only a faith but a way of life — a positive and progressive one. With the confusion that encircles the image of Islam in today's world, one can get a clearer view of the contribution of this religion to humanity, not only Muslim people, by considering how it pushed civilization forward in fast and huge leaps. Islam was revealed in an illiterate, highly ignorant society. Within decades, however, the Islamic world started to become the scientific center of the world, producing great scientists and thinkers. It studied what other various civilizations and cultures had produced, built on it, and presented to the world a new civilization that surpassed all of its predecessors and pushed the boundaries of knowledge. There is a clear, direct correlation between the embracement of Islam by the ignorant Arabs and their subsequent development of a great civilization. No other religion has had such a direct and fast positive impact on the progress of science and human civilization. The attitude of Islam toward science and knowledge is strikingly opposite to that of the Christian Church. The scientific revolution in the Christian West started only when the authority of the Church started to decline.

After this brief introduction to Islam and its history, we are ready now to start our examination of the concept of jihad in the Qur'an.

2

The Meaning of Jihad

We will start our study of jihad by investigating the general meaning of this term in the Arabic language and its special meaning in the Qur'an.

"Jihad" in the Arabic Language

The Arabic word "*jihād*" is a noun. Its singular past tense verb is "*jāhada*" (masculine) or "*jāhadat*" (feminine). The singular active participle of "jihad" is "*mujāhid*" (masculine) or "*mujāhida*" (feminine), meaning one who does jihad. The root of the word "jihad" is "*juhd*" which means "effort." Another related word is "*ijtihād*" which means "working hard or diligently."

Jihad is the process of *exerting the best efforts*, involving some form of "strife," "struggle," and resistance to something to achieve a particular goal. So jihad is the strife against or resistance to something for the sake of a goal. This meaning of the word is independent of the nature of the exerted efforts or the sought goal.

Contrary to common belief, the word "jihad" does not necessarily imply any violent effort, let alone "war" and such forms of extreme violence. It is a general term that may mean violent or peaceful actions, depending on the context in which it is used. Similarly, "jihad" as a generic word can be used even when the sought goals are not Islamic, i.e. in non-religious contexts.

The Qur'an uses the verb of "jihad" in its generic meaning of "exerting the best efforts against something" in the following two verses:

We have enjoined on man goodness to his parents, but if they *jāhadāka* (do jihad against you) to make you associate with Me [a god] of which you have no knowledge [being a god], do not obey them. To Me is your return [O people!], so I shall inform you of your past doings. (29.8).

We have enjoined on man to be good to his parents; his mother bears him in weakness upon weakness, and his weaning is in two years; that [you must] be grateful to Me and to both your parents. To Me is the eventual coming. (31.14) If they *jāhadāka* (do jihad against you) to make you associate with Me [a god] of which you have no knowledge [being a god], do not obey them, but keep kind company with them in this world; and follow the way of he who turns to Me. Then to Me is your return [O people!], then I shall inform you of your past doings. (31.15)

Jihad in these verses refers to actions taken by non-Muslim parents against their Muslim offspring to force them to worship gods other than Allah. This goal goes against the message of Islam which teaches the oneness of God. Clearly, this kind of jihad is not Islamic. These verses also confirm that jihad is not *necessarily* an act of violence.

It is worth noting that these verses command the Muslim to combine resisting any attempt by his parents to force him to give up Islamic monotheism in favor of polytheism with remaining kind and caring toward them.

"Jihad" in the Qur'an

Aside from its use of the term "jihad" in its *generic* meaning in the two verses above, the Qur'an uses "jihad" in another twenty eight verses in a *specific* meaning. In this case, the phrase "*fī sabīli Allah*" which means "in the way of Allah" or "for the sake of Allah" follows "jihad" or one of its derivatives explicitly or is implied by the context. For easy reference, Appendix A lists all thirty verses that mention the term "jihad" or any of its variations.

Contrary to the common belief that is embodied in the misinterpretation of "jihad" as "holy war," Islamic jihad does not refer solely to *fighting in the way of Allah*. This, in fact, is a special case of jihad. The Qur'anic concept of jihad denotes *exerting efforts, in the form of strife against or resistance to something, for the sake of Allah*. This effort can be fighting back armed aggression, but it can also be resisting evil drives and desires in one's self. Even donating money to the needy is a form of jihad, as it involves struggling against one's selfishness and keenness to keep any money for one's own pleasures. Jihad can, therefore, be subdivided into *armed jihad* and *peaceful jihad*. Armed jihad, which is the subject of Chapter 4, is only *temporary* and is a response to armed aggression. Once the aggression has ceased, armed jihad comes to an end. If it does not stop and continues, then it becomes aggression like the one that started the cycle of violence. Armed jihad, thus, can take place only when there is an external, aggressive enemy.

Causes of peaceful jihad, on the other hand, are always existent, which is why this form of jihad is *permanent*. One major form of peaceful jihad is the war of the Muslim against his "*nafs*" — an Arabic term that may be translated as the "lower self" and which refers to the individual's inferior drives and evil motives. This most dangerous enemy never goes away, so this war knows no end.

The other form of peaceful jihad includes any act of peaceful struggle against external sources of evil and any good effort. Preaching the message of Islam in a hostile environment, opposing an evil act, and all such peaceful good actions are instances of jihad because they involve some form of resistance and struggle to achieve a good goal. For instance, the Prophet's patience in the face of the accusations and abuse that the disbelievers directed at him for preaching the Qur'an was peaceful jihad:

> Therefore [O Muhammad!] be patient with what they say and glorify your Lord by praising Him before the rising of the sun and before its setting, and during hours of the night do also glorify [Him], and during parts of the day, that you may be well satisfied. (20.130)

It is interesting to note how the terms "jihad" and "Islam" relate to each other in Arabic and in the Qur'an. Linguistically, the general term "jihad," which refers to "struggle" and "resistance," has almost exactly the opposite meaning of the general term "Islam," which means "surrender" or "submission." But the Qur'anic "jihad," which is about resisting the lower self and other sources and forms of evil, is the route to the state of Qur'anic "Islam" or "submission to God."

Although Islamic jihad is a Qur'anic concept, the Qur'an is rarely consulted for understanding this concept. The widespread misunderstanding of jihad reflects a pandemic neglect of the Qur'an, not only by non-Muslims but by Muslims as well. The Qur'an has charged Muslims with the responsibility of educating others about its message and disseminating its teachings. Yet Muslims have had a big hand in propagating the common misunderstanding that jihad is all about violence. Many Muslims think that "jihad" means "holy war." Sadly, many Muslims learn about Islamic practices and concepts, such as jihad, from secondary, often unreliable, sources. It is not uncommon for cultural beliefs and traditions to be among those sources.

Those who misunderstand the Qur'anic term jihad as armed jihad have totally failed to notice, among other things, one particularly important fact. In the majority of verses in which the Qur'an talks about fighting the enemy, it uses variations of the word "*qitāl*," which means "fighting." Here are some examples, and we will encounter more later on:

> *Qātilū* (fight) [O you who believe!] in the way of Allah and know that Allah is Hearing, Knowing. (2.244)

> *Falyuqātil* (then let) those who sell this world's life for the hereafter (fight) in the way of Allah. Whoever *yuqātil* (fights) in the way of Allah and gets killed or turns victorious, We shall grant him a great reward. (4.74)

> *Faqātil* (then fight) [O Muhammad!] in the way of Allah. You are not held responsible but for yourself, and urge the believers [to fight]. May be Allah will restrain the might of the disbelievers. Allah is greatest in might and greatest

in punishment. (4.84)

The term jihad actually signifies the more general concept of exerting efforts in the way of God, of which fighting an aggressor, or armed jihad, is only one aspect. In Qur'anic terminology, it is wrong to equate the words "jihad" and "qitāl," as this reduces a broad concept to a more specific one.

Let's look at an example. The Qur'an refers in several verses to doing jihad with "one's property and self," i.e. sacrificing one's possessions and self in the cause of Islam, as in the following verse:

> The believers are those who believed in Allah and His Messenger, did not have doubts, and *jāhadū* (did jihad) with their property and selves in the way of Allah. These are the truthful. (49.15)

It is wrong to suggest that the verb *jāhadū* (do jihad) in this verse is equivalent to the verb *qātalū* (fight). Doing jihad with one's property and self for the sake of God covers everything that the person does to please God. Even when such efforts are in connection with a war, they would include more than the act of fighting. In other words, *jihad is more than armed jihad, which itself is more than just fighting.* Going to war means coping with the fear of getting killed or seriously injured, overcoming concerns over the family and property that the fighter leaves behind, losing earnings for being out of work during that time, and all such testing sacrifices. Braving the heat of the desert sun when traveling to and from the battle field is one aspect of armed jihad that is different from fighting itself:

> Those who were left behind were glad to sit at home and not join the Messenger of Allah. They were reluctant to *yujāhidū* (do jihad) with their property and selves and said [to other Muslims]: "Do not go forth in the heat." Say [O Muhammad!]: "The fire of Hell is far hotter," if they understand. (9.81)

The following verses make the point absolutely clear. They detail a number of different forms of hardship involved in armed jihad, with the act of fighting itself being only one of those hardships:

> It would not be fitting for the people of Medina and the Bedouin Arabs of the neighborhood to sit at home and not join the Messenger of Allah, nor should they hold themselves back from doing what he wants them to do. That is because no thirst, fatigue, or hunger afflicts them in the way of Allah; no path they tread that angers the disbelievers; and no success they achieve against an enemy but a righteous deed is written down for them on account of it. Surely, Allah does not waste the reward of the doers of good. (9.120) They do not spend anything, small or great, or cut across a valley but it is written down for them [as a credit], that Allah may reward them according to the best of their past works. (9.121)

Qitāl in the way of God is, thus, only one aspect of armed jihad. But it is the most prominent aspect and the climax of that form of jihad, which is why it is usually possible to use "qitāl in the way of God" and *armed jihad* interchangeably. Armed jihad in turn is one of two forms of jihad; the second is peaceful jihad.

So, one major aspect of the widespread misunderstanding of "jihad" is reducing it to "fighting in the way of God." What has made this confusion of "jihad" with "fighting" particularly disastrous is the equally serious misunderstanding of what constitutes legitimate fighting in Islam or "fighting in the way of God." The erroneous interpretation of the Qur'anic concept of fighting in the way of God has been extended to the Qur'anic concept of jihad. Thus, the true Qur'anic meanings of "jihad" and "fighting in the way of God" have both been distorted.

In the next chapter, we will study armed jihad. The other, more permanent form of jihad, peaceful jihad, is examined in Chapter 5.

Permission [to fight] has been granted to those against whom war is waged, because they are oppressed. Surely, Allah is well capable of assisting them [to victory].

(Qur'an, 22.39)

3

Armed Jihad: The Temporary Struggle Against the Outer Enemy

In order to understand the Qur'anic concept of armed jihad, whose main form is fighting an enemy, it is essential that we study how and why the early Muslims became involved in wars and the nature of those wars. While I will cite some explanatory historical information from outside the Qur'an for contextual purposes, the Qur'anic text will be my main source of information.

The Pre-Armed Jihad Period

For some twelve years after the revelation of the first verses of the Qur'an in 610 CE, Muslims had to endure the harshest persecution in Mecca. They had their property confiscated, were subjected to torture, and were even killed. Their only weapon was either to keep their embracement of Islam secret or, if that had already become public, endure everything with patience. Emigrating from Mecca was another option that Muslims resorted to at times, and which the Prophet himself had ultimately to choose in 622 CE as he escaped to Medina:

> If you [O people!] will not aid him [Muhammad], Allah certainly aided him when the disbelievers expelled him — he being the second of two — when they were [hiding] in the cave, when he [Muhammad] said to his companion: "Do not grieve. Surely, Allah is with us." So Allah sent down tranquility upon him, supported him with hosts that you did not see, and made lowest the word of those who disbelieved and highest the word of Allah. Allah is Invincible, Wise. (9.40)

After leaving Mecca in the night, the Prophet and his Muslim companion Abū Bakr hid for three days in a cave called "Thawr" in a mountain outside the city. When the disbelievers realized that the Prophet had fled, they went after him. They came very close to searching the cave, which is probably why Abū Bakr became so scared as shown in the verse. Tradition tells us that the chasing Qurayshites did not enter the cave because of three miracles that made the cave appear to them to have not been used for a long time: a spider weaved its web at the entrance of the cave, two wild pigeons laid eggs there, and a tree grew.

In order to be able to appreciate what this peaceful struggle of

Muslims, which later led to their immigration, really meant, it is essential to know the circumstances in which it took place.

The people of the Arabian Peninsula were very violent. Raids amongst tribes were a common way of increasing both wealth and social standing. In that bloody environment, vengeance and retaliation were major drives in people's lives. Embracing Islam meant turning one's back on such practices. In the first fourteen years of Muhammad's mission, Muslims as a group did not take part in any war. The Prophet and his followers could only use peaceful means even in response to the harshest forms of persecution. It is reported that Muslims who were beaten or tortured for embracing Islam would ask the Prophet for permission to defend themselves, but he would reply that God had not given permission for Muslims to take arms. He would console them, remind them of the virtues of patience, give them hope, and offer them advice on how to avoid and/or mitigate the persecution they were subjected to.

This was a great test that God put early Muslims through. Passing that trial required challenging so many established traditions and beliefs of the society in which Muslims were born and raised. They set a noble example that the Arabs, and indeed peoples of the time in general, had never seen or heard of before. In order to be able to follow the new religion, the individual would have to undergo a rebirth and total renewal of himself. Those who were not genuinely willing to change could not become Muslims. This self-control is peaceful jihad. Peaceful jihad started long before armed jihad.

The Qur'an gives us a fascinating insight into the extent of the peaceful jihad that the early Muslims had to practice to meet the requirements of Islam. Those Arab converts came from different tribes with a long history of enmity between them. They had to erase their attachment to that pre-Islamic past and its tradition, embrace the present and its new values, and relate to each other in a completely different way. They were no more sworn enemies, but close brothers and sisters who were willing to sacrifice themselves for each other. The Qur'an describes this transformation as a miracle:

> Hold fast [O you who believe!] — all of you together — to the rope of Allah, and do not be divided among yourselves. Remember Allah's favor to you; how you were enemies but He established affection between your hearts, so that by His favor you have become brethren. And you were on the brink of the pit of Fire, but He saved you from it. Thus Allah makes His signs clear to you that you may be guided. (3.103)

> If they (the disbelievers) intend to deceive you [O Muhammad!], then surely Allah is sufficient for you. It is He who supported you with His help and with the believers (8.62) and established affection between their hearts. Even if

you had spent all that is on earth you would not have established affection between their hearts, but Allah established affection between them. Surely, He is Mighty, Wise. (8.63)

God reminds the Prophet that had he relied on his own effort, he could not have turned those enemies into brothers even if he had all of the earth's riches to do that. It was a divine miracle that achieved that.

The Divine Permission for Armed Jihad

In the second year after the immigration of the Prophet to Medina, i.e. about fourteen years after the revelation of the Qur'an, God granted the Muslims permission to use force to defend themselves. Muslims could now fight back to protect themselves and their property; they have become entitled to armed jihad. Most scholars consider verse 22.39 to be the first verse that granted Muslims the right to carry arms to defend themselves against their attackers. This is the permission verse, along with verses that precede and follow it:

Surely, Allah defends those who believe. Surely, Allah does not love anyone who is unfaithful, ungrateful. (22.38) Permission [to fight] has been granted to those against whom war is waged, because they are oppressed. Surely, Allah is well capable of assisting them [to victory]. (22.39) [The permission is to] those who have been driven out of their homes without a just cause, only because they say: "Our Lord is Allah." Had it not been for Allah's repelling some people by means of others, then certainly cloisters, churches, synagogues, and mosques in which Allah's name is much remembered would have been pulled down. Surely, Allah will help him who helps His cause. Surely, Allah is Mighty, Invincible. (22.40) [The permission is to] those who, should We establish them in the land, will keep up prayer, pay the obligatory alms, enjoin good, and forbid evil. Allah's is the sequel of events. (22.41)

Note the justification for granting the Muslims the right to armed jihad. They were allowed to fight back those who had *waged war against them* and *driven them out of their homes*. Armed jihad is obviously a permission for armed *self-defense*.

The following verse confirms that Muslims had wanted to defend themselves but were prevented by the Prophet because at that point God had not granted them permission to fight back. This reminder was clearly revealed after the believers were given the right to defend themselves:

Have you not seen [O Muhammad!] those to whom it was said: "Withhold your hands [from fighting], keep up prayer, and pay the obligatory alms," when fighting was ordained on them, a party of them feared people as they ought to fear Allah or [even] with a greater fear, and said: "Our Lord! Why have You ordained fighting on us? If You have only granted us a delay to a near date?" Say [O Muhammad!]: "The provision of this world is short, and the hereafter is better for he who acts dutifully toward Allah; and you shall not be wronged in the very least." (4.77)

God's promise in verse 22.39 that He will grant the Muslims victory is remarkable. At the time, the Muslims were a very small minority whose enemy was almost everyone in that region. It suffices to know that in their first major battle against the disbelievers, which is known as the battle of Badr after its location, the Muslim army reportedly consisted of only three hundred and thirteen men. The fact that the victorious Muslim fighters were a much smaller army than their defeated enemy is documented in the Qur'an:

Surely, Allah assisted you [O believers!] to victory at Badr when you were vulnerable. So be pious to Allah so that you may give thanks [to Him]. (3.123)

The fulfillment of the promise of victory in verse 22.39 is one miracle that attests to the divine source of that promise and, therefore, of the Qur'an.

Verse 22.40 stresses that had God not instructed people to defend themselves, their right to worship would have been eroded as "cloisters, churches, synagogues, and mosques" would have been destroyed. Significantly, God does not differentiate between those places, treating them equally as places of worship. Rather than aggression to deprive people of their freedom, as portrayed in its popularized image, armed jihad is a just struggle for freedom and basic human rights.

Some scholars believe that while verse 22.39 granted the Muslims permission to fight back, it did not make fighting *obligatory*. These scholars differentiate between this *permission* and the *command* in other, later verses for Muslims to fight:

Fighting has been ordained on you [O you who believe!], and it is an object of dislike to you; and it may be that you dislike a thing while it is good for you, and it may be that you love a thing while it is evil for you; and Allah knows whereas you do not know. (2.216)

The following verse states that those who practiced armed jihad and spent some of their money in the cause of God were better than those who chose not to despite having no physical disability or lacking means:

Not equal are the believers who have no impediment yet sit at home and *al-mujāhidūna* (those who do jihad) in the way of Allah with their property and selves. Allah has favored *al-mujāhidīna* (those who do jihad) with their property and selves over those who sit at home with a higher degree; and Allah has promised good to both. Allah has favored *al-mujāhidīna* (those who do jihad) over those who sit at home with a mighty reward. (4.95)

Interestingly, the verse does not condemn those who chose to sit at home but only gives them a lower standing in God's sight and promises them less rewards in the hereafter. Verse 9.120 (p. 26) also stresses that Muslims had to fight with the Prophet but does not chastise those who failed to do so. Probably there were times when fighting was a strict obligation on Muslims.

The fact that hostilities between the Muslims and their enemies started as a result of the aggression of the latter is seen in this verse also:

> O you who believe! Do not take My enemy and your enemy for guardians, offering them love while they have rejected what has come to you of the truth, having driven out the Messenger and you because you believe in Allah, your Lord — if you have gone forth *jihādan* (doing jihad) in My way and seeking My pleasure. You show love to them in private, and I know what you conceal and what you reveal. Whoever of you does this, he indeed has gone astray from the straight path. (60.1)

This verse warns the Muslims against establishing friendly relationships with people who cannot be trusted, having shown so much enmity toward the Prophet and other Muslims.

A Means to Peace

The Qur'an focuses on developing human society and instilling moral values, but it does not indulge in any attempt to establish an unrealistic utopia on earth. Paradise is the Qur'an's ideal world. While it ultimately promotes peace, it makes it also clear that peaceful actions alone would not be enough to lead to peace. Human experience and history show that it is preposterous to think that peace can be achieved and maintained by peaceful means only. There are many circumstances where violence and war are the only route to peace. So the ultimate goal of armed jihad is to establish peace.

Verses 22.39-40 show clearly that armed jihad is a defensive rather than offensive form of struggle. It is about defending one's self and property against aggression and one's freedom and human rights against oppression. This is emphasized in so many verses throughout the Qur'an. It is well illustrated in the fact that Muslims are not permitted to fight anyone who is willing to offer them peace. Let's look, for example, at what God says about the renegades who embraced Islam but later reverted to their old religion:

> They (the hypocrites) desire that you [O you who believe!] disbelieve as they have disbelieved, so that you might be all alike. Therefore, do not take from among them guardians until they immigrate in the way of Allah. But if they turn away, then seize and kill them wherever you find them, and do not take from among them a guardians or a helper, (4.89) except those who have a connection with a people with whom you have a treaty [of peace] or who come to you with their hearts constricted from fighting you or fighting their

own people. Had Allah wanted, He would have sent them on you so that they would have fought you. Therefore, if they withdraw so they do not fight you and they offer you peace, then Allah has not made for you a case [to wage war] against them. (4.90) You will find others who wish to have security from you and security from their own people yet whenever tempted back to mischief they plunge into it. Therefore, if they do not withdraw, offer you peace, and restrain their hands, seize and kill them wherever you get hold of them. It is against these that We have given you a clear authority [to fight]. (4.91)

God commands the Muslims to fight, in addition to the disbelievers who have declared war against them, the hypocrites who rejoined the forces of disbelievers and fought against the Muslims after being with them. Significantly, He excludes two groups of those hypocrites.

The first group consists of those who had some relation with a people with whom Muslims had made peace. Muslims are disallowed to fight not only the people they have signed a peace treaty with, but also people who are connected to the signatories to peace. This shows the extent to which the Qur'an promotes and encourages peace.

The second group of hypocrites includes those who decline to take sides in the war between their people and the Muslims. God commands the Muslims not to fight those *who withdraw, do not fight them, and offer them peace*. Note the contrast between these tolerant commands and the popular misconception that Islam punishes or even kills the Muslims who reject their religion.

As for those who side with their people against the Muslims, don't offer peace, and don't restrain their hands, God has given the Muslims a clear authority to fight them. It is clear that armed jihad is *defensive reaction rather than offensive action*.

There are many references in the Qur'an instructing the Prophet and the Muslims to establish peace with any enemy once that enemy became interested in peace. Let's have a look at another set of verses:

Surely, the worst of beasts in Allah's sight are those who are ungrateful as they would not believe. (8.55) Those with whom you [O Muhammad!] have made a covenant yet they break their covenant every time and do not act piously. (8.56) Therefore, should you get hold of them in war, make of them an example that would disperse [the gathering army of] those who are behind them that they may be mindful. (8.57) If you fear treachery from a people, then throw back to them [their treaty] on equal terms. Surely, Allah does not love the treacherous. (8.58) Let not those who disbelieve think that they can outstrip [Us]. Surely, they are not impregnable. (8.59) Prepare [O you who believe!] for them what you can of force and horses tethered, to frighten thereby Allah's and your enemy and others besides them whom you do not know but Allah knows. Whatever you spend in the way of Allah will be paid back to you in full and you shall not be wronged. (8.60) If they incline to peace then incline [O Muhammad!] to it, and rely on Allah. Surely, He is the

Hearing, the Knowing. (8.61) If they intend to deceive you, then surely Allah is sufficient for you. It is He who supported you with His help and with the believers. (8.62)

Verse 8.56 talks about those who *repeatedly* violated their peace treaty with the Muslims. This does not only show the untrustworthiness and treacherousness of the people that Muslims had to make peace with, but it also evinces the keenness of the Muslims on peace. Prophet Muhammad was willing to reinstate the peace he had with other people even though the latter had breached it a number of times. If that violation of the peace treaty continued, the Prophet is given in verse 8.58 the permission not to honor what had effectively become an abolished and worthless treaty.

God's command to the Muslims to make of the enemy *an example that would disperse the gathered armies of other disbelievers* emphasizes the fact that armed jihad is used as *a means to avert more wars and aggression*. This is also embodied in God's command to Muslims in verse 8.60 to prepare what they can "of force and horses tethered" in order to *frighten* the *enemies they knew and others they didn't*.

After highlighting the nature of betrayal and perfidy of the disbelievers, God goes on to give the following amazing command to the Muslims: "If they incline to peace then incline to it, and rely on Allah." Despite those peoples' history of savage aggression against Muslims, the latter are ordered to opt for peace should their enemies become interested in peace. This divine command teaches a kind of commitment to peace that is extraordinary by any standards. The Prophet would have felt apprehensive about agreeing peace with people who had repeatedly broken their word. This is why God commands the Prophet to rely on Him and reminds him that He hears and knows everything. He then goes on to reassure the Prophet in the next verse that He is on his side should those people resort to deception: "If they intend to deceive you, then surely Allah is sufficient for you." Allah then reminds His Messenger how He supported him with "His help and with the believers." Clearly, armed jihad in Islam is not about vengeance. It is the kind of armed struggle that can be truly and fairly described as a *war for peace*.

At the time of the events above, vengeance was, and is largely still, a major drive for wars and acts of aggression. Those early Muslims were born and brought up in an environment where lengthy, full-blown wars would be started for the most trivial of reasons. Tribes and individuals used to inherit and pass bloody grudges from one generation to another. For instance, the killing of a she-camel started the war of "al-Basūs" between the clans of Taghlib and Bakr which lasted for 40 years (494-534

CE)! The clans of 'Abs and Dhubyān fought another famous war that also lasted for four decades. This time, the bloody war was started by a disagreement on a race between two horses, "Dāḥis" and "al-Ghabrā'," after which the war was named! This shows how difficult and challenging the divine command to refrain from seeking revenge was.

One remarkable example is the Muslim's *peaceful* conquest of Mecca eight years after the Prophet and Muslims were forced out of it, escaping death and torture and, in doing so, losing all their possessions. In those eight years, the Qurayshites of Mecca did not stop their persecution of the immigrant Muslims in Medina, keeping them in an almost continuous state of war. Nevertheless, when the Muslim army entered Mecca truly non-violently, the Prophet issued an amnesty for all of its people, regardless of what they had done to Muslims over the years. Seventeen people were excluded from the amnesty, but most of them were also later pardoned. Only four were killed for their particularly heinous crimes. Most probably, the killing of those four spared the shedding of further blood.

The Prophet didn't seek to exact revenge even on the most evil people, some of whom had caused him personally great pain and suffering. One such person was a woman called "Hind bint 'Utba." A few years earlier, she hired a slave to kill the Prophet's uncle, "Ḥamza," who was also one of his closest companions. Her hatred for the Prophet and Muslims was such that she cannibalized Ḥamza's liver and was involved in mutilating Muslim martyrs. When Hind bint 'Utba came to visit the Prophet after the conquest of Mecca to declare her embracement of Islam, he couldn't even look at her face, as it reminded him of her crimes which were still painful to him. Even this woman escaped punishment.

These are great lessons in obeying God's command of forgiveness. This is how the Prophet taught peaceful jihad by example as well as word.

Let's study another set of verses that shed light on the causes of the conflict between the Muslims and the disbelievers:

If anyone of the polytheists seeks your protection [O Muhammad!], then protect him so that he may hear the Word of Allah, and escort him to his place of safety. That is because they are a people who do not know. (9.6) How can there be a treaty with Allah and with His Messenger for the polytheists, save those with whom you [O you who believe!] made a treaty with at the Inviolable Mosque? So long as they are true to you, be true to them. Surely, Allah loves the pious. (9.7) How [can there be any treaty for the others] when, if they would get an advantage over you, they would not honor any relation or treaty with you? They satisfy you with their mouths, while their hearts refuse. Most of them are backsliders. (9.8) They have purchased with the verses of Allah a little gain, so they turned away from His way. Surely, evil is what they do. (9.9) They do not honor any relation or treaty with a believer;

these are the transgressors. (9.10) But if they repent, establish regular prayers, and pay the obligatory alms, then they are your brethren in religion. We detail Our verses for the people of knowledge. (9.11) If they break their oaths after their treaty [with you] and assail your religion, then fight the heads of disbelief. Surely, they have no binding oaths, so that they may desist. (9.12) Will you not fight a people who broke their oaths and set out to drive out the Messenger and they attacked you first? Do you fear them? Allah is more worthy of your fear, if you are believers. (9.13)

The first verse shows that Islam does not consider a peaceful disbeliever an enemy. The Qur'an even commanded the Prophet to give protection to any polytheist who sought his help.

Verse 9.7 commands the Muslims to honor their treaty with the polytheists as long as the latter honored it. God considers this to be an act of piety: "Allah loves the pious." He reminds the Muslims in verses 9.8-10 that the polytheists used to break their peace treaties whenever they felt they had the upper hand and that they showed a similar disregard for their relations with the Muslims. He explains that the polytheists made peace with their mouths but did not embrace it with their hearts.

Muslims were commanded to forgive the polytheists, live with them in peace if the latter honored peace, and forgive and consider them brothers if they convert to Islam (9.11). God (9.12) then emphasizes that the aim of fighting the heads of disbelief is to make them desist and establish peace.

Finally, verse 9.13 urges the Muslims to fight aggression, reminding them of the background of the conflict with the disbelievers. **First**, it was the polytheists who broke the treaty they had with the Muslims. **Second**, like the Meccans who forced the Prophet to immigrate to Medina, the polytheists were trying to expel him from Medina. **Third**, it was the polytheists who attacked the Muslims first.

I would like to quote one more verse that shows the keenness of Muslims on having peace with non-Muslims and honoring that peace:

Surely, those who believed, immigrated, and *jāhadū* [did jihad] with their property and selves in the way of Allah and those who gave shelter [to the immigrants] and helped them are guardians of each other. As for those who believed but did not immigrate, you [O you who believe!] have no duty of guardianship toward them until they immigrate. If they seek help from you for the purpose of religion, then help is incumbent on you, except helping them against a people with whom you have a treaty. Allah sees what you do. (8.72)

The immigrant Muslims from Mecca were well received by their fellow believers in Medina who gave them shelter and shared their belongings with them. In the verse above, God makes a clear distinction between those immigrant Muslims and others elsewhere who did not respond to the divine command to immigrate to Medina. The verse tells the Muslims in Medina that they are guardians of each other, but not of those Muslims who had not emigrated to join them. What is particularly relevant to our current discussion is God's order in the second half of the verse. The Muslims who did not emigrate could be attacked because of their religion, in which case they might ask for help from their brothers in Medina. That help would come only if the aggressors had no peace treaty with the Prophet. If those non-Muslims were in peace with the Prophet, the Muslims of Medina would not attack them and the call for help from the non-immigrant Muslims would go unheeded. There are two important points to highlight here.

First, the Muslims honored their peace pacts. Those who attack Muslims because of their religion are, obviously, not friendly to Islam, let alone believers in its cause. But this enmity would not prevent the Muslims from seeking peace with those people. This means that Muslims never forced Islam on anyone and they were honest and truthful in seeking to live in peace even with those who disliked their religion. They resorted to war only when the other party showed no interest in peace and insisted on aggression.

Second, the verse leaves no doubt whatsoever that the Qur'an doesn't permit the involvement in a war that can be averted. The war against those non-immigrant Muslims was not unavoidable. Had those Muslims immigrated to Medina, they would have been spared the aggression they suffered, because their persecutors had already agreed peace with the Muslims of Medina. There was a way to avoid war, which is to immigrate to Medina, hence the intervention of the Muslims of Medina was not forthcoming. However, if the non-immigrant Muslims had asked for help against aggressors who had not agreed peace with the Muslims of Medina, the latter would have responded, because that would have been an unavoidable war. If the aggressors had any interest in peace, they would have agreed peace with the Muslims of Medina.

Prohibiting Aggression and Enjoining Forgiveness

While granted permission from God to fight back their attackers, Muslims are reminded in many verses that they should never commit aggression even against their sworn enemies. Their response must not be disproportionate or go beyond the limits of the permission for armed jihad:

> Let not hatred of a people, having prevented you [O you who believe!] from visiting the Inviolable Mosque, cause you to commit transgression. Help one another in [practicing] righteousness and piety, and do not help one another in [committing] sin and transgression. Be pious to Allah. Surely, Allah is severe in punishment. (from 5.2)

O you who believe! Stand firm for Allah, [as] witnesses with justice. Let not hatred of a people cause you not to act equitably; act equitably; that is nearer to piety. Be pious to Allah. Surely, Allah is aware of what you do. (5.8)

Fight in the way of Allah those who fight you [O you who believe!], and do not transgress. Surely, Allah does not love the aggressors. (2.190) Kill them wherever you find them and drive them out whence they drove you out; persecution is severer than killing. Do not fight them at the Inviolable Mosque until they fight you in it, but if they do fight you, then kill them. Such is the reward of the disbelievers. (2.191) But if they desist, then surely Allah is Forgiving, Merciful. (2.192) Fight them until there is no persecution and religion is Allah's. But if they desist, then there should be no hostility, except against the wrongdoers. (2.193)

Verse 2.190 reiterates the fact that Muslims were granted permission to resort to armed jihad against those who attack them. Muslims were simply defending themselves. These verses make it clear that it was the disbelievers who started all forms of hostilities and that stopping the aggression was in their hands. Muslims were only responding to the aggressors, and doing so in a measured way.

Verse 2.192 stresses that God remains forgiving and willing to offer mercy to the disbelievers if they quit their hostilities. This is not only a message to the disbelievers encouraging them to resort to peace, but it is also a clear instruction to the Muslims that the end of hostilities means no lingering grudges or seeking of revenge. Since God offers forgiveness and mercy to the sinful when they repent, Muslims must respond to the ceasing of hostilities with forgiveness and mercy for their enemy.

Let's look at another relevant set of verses. Addressing the believers, verse 42.36 belittles whatever can be earned in this world and encourages the believers to aspire more toward the rewards of the hereafter: "So whatever you are given, that is only a provision of this world's life. What is with Allah is better and more lasting for those who believe and rely on their Lord." God then goes on to talk about qualities of the believers and give them more instructions:

[What is with the Lord is better for] those who avoid the greater sins and indecencies, and when they get angry they forgive; (42.37) who respond to [the call of] their Lord, keep up prayer, manage their affairs by mutual consultation, and spend out of what We bestow on them; (42.38) and who, when wronged, help each other [against the aggressor]. (42.39) The recompense of an act of aggression is a similar act, so whoever forgives and makes reconciliation then he will have his rewards from Allah. Surely, He does not love the wrongdoers. (42.40) As for those who help each other [against the aggressor] after they have been oppressed, Allah has not made a case against them. (42.41) The case is rather against those who wrong people and exercise oppression unjustly on earth; those shall have a painful punishment. (42.42) As for showing patience and forgiveness, these are surely actions of determination. (42.43)

The fact that Muslims got involved in wars because they were oppressed is made clear in verse 42.39. God stresses in verse 42.41 that defending one's self against oppression is not a sin. The sinful people, verse 42.42 states, are those who wrong and oppress other people. Significantly, this set of verses starts and ends with instructions urging Muslims to forgive. God's message to the Muslims is to fight back when war is waged against them, but to stop all hostilities and forgive their former enemies when peace is reached.

Contrary to its popular image among those who have not studied it, the Qur'an always enjoins Muslims to forgive. It also states that when patience and forgiveness are an option, they are better than retaliation. The following verses order the Muslims to forgive the People of the Book who were as hostile to the new religion as the Qurayshites, with some Jews even establishing with the latter at one point a war alliance against the Muslims:

> But because of their breach of their covenant We cursed them and made their hearts hard: they altered words from their contexts, and they forgot a part of what they were reminded of. You [O Muhammad!] will continue to discover treachery from them, save a minority of them. So pardon them and overlook [their misdeeds]. Surely, Allah loves those who do charity. (5.13)

> Many of the People of the Book wish that they could turn you [O you who believe!] back into disbelievers after you have believed, out of envy, [even] after the truth has become manifest to them. So, forgive and overlook [their misdeeds] until Allah brings about His judgment. Surely, Allah has power over all things. (2.109)

God's command to the Muslims not to transgress — which is stated explicitly in 5.2, 5.8, 2.190, 2.193, 42.40, and other verses — stresses a number of points. **First**, Muslims must not fight someone who has not chosen to fight them. They must not launch premeditated, preemptive, or unprovoked attacks. **Second**, when they respond to aggression, their response must be in line with the rules that govern armed jihad. For instance, if the aggressors genuinely decided at some point to opt for peace, Muslims must take the route of peace immediately. **Third**, the Muslims' response to any hostility must be proportionate and measured. Any failure to apply this would result in the once victims becoming, according to the Qur'an, aggressors themselves. Let's study the third point in more detail.

Measured and Proportionate Retaliation

This is one verse that teaches Muslims to be measured in their response to aggression:

> The [violation of] an Inviolable Month is for [the violation of] an Inviolable Month, and the violation of anything is retaliated to with the same. So, whoever commits a hostility against you [O you who believe!], respond to him with a similar hostility. Be pious to Allah, and know that Allah is with the pious. (2.194)

The Arabs before Islam used to observe total peace in four months of the year known as the *al-Ḥurum* or Inviolable Months. If enemies of Islam violated one of these months and attacked Muslims, this verse instructs the Muslims to retaliate within that month only. Muslims must not continue the hostilities into another Inviolable Month unless their enemies start new hostilities in that month. The verse states that all retaliatory acts by Muslims must be characterized by measuredness and proportionality.

We can see a similar example in verse 2.191, which addresses the Muslims saying: "Do not fight them at the Inviolable Mosque until they fight you in it, but if they do fight you, then kill them." Because the Inviolable Mosque, which is the mosque surrounding the Ka'ba, is a place in which fighting is prohibited, Muslims were not allowed to attack their enemies with whom they were at war. They were permitted to fight at the Inviolable Mosque only if their enemies extended the fighting to that place. Once the enemies have stopped hostilities in the Inviolable Mosque, the Muslims must cease fighting there immediately. God's commands aim at containing hostilities and limiting them.

In addition to commanding Muslims to be measured in their responses to aggression, the following verse encourages people to forgive and seek reconciliation:

> The recompense of an act of aggression is a similar act, so whoever forgives and makes reconciliation then he will have his rewards from Allah. Surely, He does not love the wrongdoers. (42.40)

This is another verse that orders the Muslims to respond to aggression proportionately, and it also urges them to forgive, stating that responding with patience instead of retaliating — when this is an option — is better:

> If you punish [O you who believe!], then punish like you were punished. If you show patience, then it is better for the patient. (16.126)

Again, putting these divine instructions in their historical context shows how revolutionary they were. This unique, divine justice is one aspect of the beauty of the Qur'an and its Lord, Allah.

Its genuine measuredness and proportionality make the military response in Islam in complete contrast to modern wars. The overwhelming majority of human casualties in modern wars are not intended targets. This is the result of the use of weapons of mass destruction which are becoming increasingly deadlier. Those mass killing machines are not restricted, as their manufacturers and users would have us believe, to nuclear, chemical, and biological weapons. Any weapon that cannot be used effectively to select its intended target is a blind, mass killing piece of weaponry. A *classical* bomb or rocket, therefore, is effectively a weapon of mass destruction though not labeled as such.

Furthermore, given enough numbers of such conventional weapons and the difference between them and weapons of mass destruction would be nonexistent. This is testified to by the hundreds of thousands of innocent victims in Palestine, Iraq, Afghanistan, and other places that were subjected to the horror of those supposedly less devastating weapons. Modern war strategies, such as "carpet bombing" that was used to devastating effects against Vietnam, have ensured that the difference in destruction and brutality between classical and non-classical wars is practically nonexistent.

As if these blind and deadly weapons, which are launched far from their intended targets and which kill numerous invisible people, are not satisfying enough, an even *cleaner* and *neater* mass killing weapon called "economic sanctions" was commissioned against Iraq in the 1990s. This weapon proved particularly successful in murdering children, the elderly, the ill, and the poor. The deadly irony is that these sanctions, we are told, were put in place to prevent Iraq from developing weapons of mass destruction!

There is a fundamental difference between the controlled and targeted retaliation that the Qur'an permits and the emotive, disproportionate, and indiscriminate actions that characterize wars in general.

Warning Against the Abuse of Armed Jihad

As we have seen, God has warned, in general terms, Muslims against abusing the permission He granted them to defend themselves. He has also mentioned particular cases of abuse that may happen and warned against them:

> O you who believe! When you travel in the way of Allah, investigate and do not say to someone who offers you peace: "You are not a believer," seeking riches of this world, for with Allah there are abundant spoils. You too were so before, then Allah conferred favors on you. So investigate. Allah is aware of what you do. (4.94)

Muslims who travelled inside or outside Arabia during times of war would come across non-Muslims previously unknown to them. Some of these non-Muslims would be potential enemies who would raise their arms in the face of Muslims. Others would be interested in peaceful co-existence with Muslims.

Verse 4.94 urges Muslims to investigate whether the people they encounter are potential enemies or not. It then goes on to warn against a particular evil temptation that some Muslims may be susceptible to. Some of the strangers that traveling Muslims would meet would offer peace. Some Muslims may be tempted to reject that offer on the basis that it came from non-Muslims, treat them as enemies, kill them, and take their belongings as spoils of war. Those who commit such aggression would portray it as something they did for the sake of God, which is the implication of their words to the victim: "You are not a believer." God has exposed this claim as a false pretext and revealed that the real drive behind this act of aggression is "seeking riches of this world." He reminds those Muslims that they should seek the eternal rewards that He has prepared for the righteous people in the hereafter not those illegitimately obtained worldly riches.

By saying to the non-Muslim "You are not a believer," those Muslims imply that they are superior. In rejecting this attitude, God reminds the Muslims that they also were disbelievers in the past and that it is due to His favor they are now Muslims: "You too were so before, then Allah conferred favors on you." Had God not guided the Muslims to Islam, they would have remained disbelievers.

God also implies that He did not give permission to anyone to kill the now Muslims before they embraced Islam, so how could they justify killing non-Muslims simply for not embracing Islam? Additionally, how can they ascertain that today's disbelievers would not become Muslims in the future, as happened with them?

To stress the message, God reminds the Muslims again near the end of the verse that they must investigate carefully the state of the strangers they encounter before taking any action. Finally, there is a reminder that God knows everything that people do, meaning that Muslims must not forget that He is aware of the way they behave in any situation including the one described in the verse. Trying to deceive God is not an option.

Note the fairness and impartiality of the Qur'an as it highlights a temptation that some Muslims may fall victim to. Qur'anic justice is based on clear principles that are applied equally. The Qur'an does not compromise on principles, regardless of the parties involved. It contains no form of favoritism. It criticizes errant Muslims as it does with non-Muslims.

The Qur'an goes even further than that. While it calls those who don't embrace Islam "disbelievers," it describes Muslims who embrace Islam in name only "hypocrites" and considers the latter far worse than the disbelievers. The disbelievers will be punished with Hell, whereas the hypocrites are destined to the lowest places in Hell:

> Surely, the hypocrites will be in the lowest depth of the Fire, and you shall not find a helper for them. (4.145)

The Prohibition of Forcing People into Islam

Contrary to what many believe, armed jihad is not meant to force people into Islam. There are many Qur'anic verses, some of which we have already studied, that order Muslims to live in peace with any peaceful people, whether Muslims or not. This is clear, for instance, in the following verses:

> Allah does not forbid you [O you who believe!] from being kind and just to those who have not waged war against you because of your religion and have not driven you out of your homes. Surely, Allah loves those who are just. (60.8) He only forbids you from taking guardians those who have waged war against you because of your religion, have driven you out of your homes, and have supported others in driving you out. As to those who take them as guardians, these are the wrongdoers. (60.9)

The enemies of Muslims are not non-Muslims, but those who have waged war against them and have driven them out of their homes for embracing Islam. Significantly, God orders the Muslims to be "kind" and "just" to the non-Muslims who did not take part in violence against them. These verses remove any possible ambiguity and misunderstanding as to how Muslims should treat non-Muslims who are willing to live in peace with them and how Muslims should identify and treat their enemies.

God has explicitly prohibited coercing people into faith saying: "there is no compulsion in religion" (from 2.256). Elsewhere in the Qur'an, God mentions this prayer of complaint by the Prophet: "O my Lord! Surely, they are a people who do not believe" (from 43.88), before revealing His reply to the Messenger: "So turn away from them and say "peace," for they shall come to know" (43.89). God instructed the Prophet to turn away from the disbelievers on peaceful terms, reminding him that they will come to know on the Day of Judgment that what they rejected is the truth.

I will quote below more verses that instruct the Prophet to turn away from the disbelievers who are not interested in his message. Forcing people to adopt Islam was never an option:

> Follow [O Muhammad!] what has been revealed to you from your Lord. There is no god but He. Turn away from the polytheists. (6.106)

Therefore turn away [O Muhammad!] from him who turns aside from Our Reminder (the Qur'an) and does not desire anything but this world's life. (53.29) That is as much knowledge as they will get. Surely, your Lord knows best those who have gone astray from His path, and He knows best the guided ones. (53.30)

Therefore, declare [O Muhammad!] publicly what you are commanded and turn away from the polytheists. (15.94) Surely, We will suffice you against the scoffers (15.95) — those who set another god with Allah. They shall come to know. (15.96) Surely, We know that your heart is distressed by what they say. (15.97) Therefore, celebrate the praise of your Lord and be one of those who make prostration [to Him]. (15.98)

There are many verses that make it clear that the role of the Prophet was to *deliver the divine message*, that is the Qur'an, to people. The Prophet warned the disbelievers of Hell and brought good news to the believers. He was not a "controller" or "keeper" over people, and he was not to answer for their disbelief. These are some relevant verses:

Those who disbelieve say: "If only a sign had been sent down upon him (Muhammad) from his Lord." You are not [O Muhammad!] but a warner and for every people a guide. (13.7)

Surely, We have sent you [O Muhammad!] with truth, as a bearer of good news and a warner. You shall not be called upon to answer for the people of Hell. (2.119)

Surely, We have revealed to you [O Muhammad!] the Book for the people with truth. So whoever follows the right way, it is for his own soul, and whoever goes astray, he goes astray only to its detriment. You have not been put in charge of them. (39.41)

Had Allah willed, they (the disbelievers) would not have associated gods with Allah. We have not appointed you [O Muhammad!] as a keeper over them and you have not been put in charge of them. (6.107)

Whoever obeys the Messenger, he has indeed obeyed Allah. As for he who turns away, We have not sent you [O Muhammad!] as a keeper over them. (4.80)

Therefore, do [O Muhammad!] remind [with the message] for you are only a reminder. (88.21) You are not a controller over them. (88.22)

We know best what they say [about Our revelation to you, O Muhammad!], and you are not to be a dictator over them. Therefore, remind by the Qur'an him who fears My threat. (50.45)

But if they turn away, then We have not sent you [O Muhammad!] as a keeper over them. Only deliverance [of the Message] is your duty. (from 42.48)

If you [O disbelievers!] deny [the truth], then nations before you also denied [it]. Nothing is incumbent on the Messenger other than plain deliverance [of the Message]. (29.18)

Whether We show you [O Muhammad!] part of what We threaten them (the disbelievers) with or cause you to die, [only] deliverance [of the Message] is your duty, while calling [the disbelievers] to account is Our business. (13.40)

The Qur'an teaches that attracting people to Islam must occur through good-mannered preaching and discussion:

Call [O Muhammad!] to the way of your Lord with wisdom and goodly exhortation and argue with them in the best manner. Surely, your Lord best knows those who go astray from His path, and He best knows those who follow the right way. (16.125)

Clearly, peaceful rather than armed jihad is the Qur'anic way of calling people to Islam. I will talk about this more in the next chapter.

As well as prohibiting the forcing of people to embrace Islam, the Qur'an has also made it clear that other religions can coexist with Islam. This tolerance includes even religions that Islam does not consider to be genuine, such as pagan faiths. This Meccan chapter carries instructions to Prophet Muhammad to seek peaceful coexistence with the polytheistic Qurayshites:

Say [O Muhammad!]: "O disbelievers! (109.1) I do not worship that which you worship, (109.2) nor do you worship that which I worship, (109.3) nor I shall worship that which you worship, (109.4) nor do you worship that which I worship. (109.5) You have your religion and I have mine." (109.6)

The situation in Medina was similar. Muslims sought peaceful coexistence with the People of the Book. There are many verses that show various theological discussions and debates that were taking place between Muslims and followers of Judaism and Christianity. The Qur'an promised Paradise to all those who believe in God and the Day of Judgment and do good works, whether they were Jews, Christians, Sabaeans, or Muslims:

Those who believe, the Jews, the Christians, and the Sabaeans — whoever believe in Allah and the Last day and do good — they shall have their reward from their Lord, and there is no fear for them nor shall they grieve. (5.69)

Relations between the Muslims and the Jews in Medina deteriorated only when the latter got involved in the Qurayshites' wars and conspiracies against the Muslims. Muslims had to fight the Jews for the same reasons that they had to fight the polytheistic Meccans: defending their right to choose Islam as their religion.

The fact that Jews, Christians, and believers of other faiths lived safely under Islam and were allowed to practice their religions reflects the tolerance of the Qur'an:

After Muhammad's death, Jews and Christians were never required to convert to Islam but were allowed to practice their religions freely in the Islamic empire. Later Zoroastrians, Hindus, Buddhists and Sikhs were also counted among the People of the Book. It has never been a problem for Muslims to coexist with people of other religions. The Islamic empire was able to play host to Christians and Jews for centuries; but Western Europe has found it almost impossible to tolerate Muslims and Jews in Christian territory. (Armstrong, 2001: 87)

This Qur'anic tolerance toward other religions, which history tells us Muslims applied wherever they ruled, is in complete contradiction with the image of extremism and intolerance of Islam in the West today. But fundamentalist Muslims, whose ignorance of Islam developed into extremism or terrorism, have contributed in a big way to this unfounded presentation of Islam.

The Qur'an differentiates between those non-Muslim believers who fought the Prophet and his followers and those who chose to live peacefully with and accommodate them. It goes as far as putting the latter and the Muslims in one group, describing them as citizens of one nation it calls *khyara umma* or "best nation":

> You have been the best nation that has been raised up for mankind. You enjoin what is right, forbid what is wrong, and believe in Allah. If the People of the Book believe [in Islam], it would be better for them; there are believers among them, but most of them are backsliders. (3.110) They will not harm you but a slight hurt. If they fight you, they shall turn their backs to you [to flee], and they shall not be helped. (3.111) Abasement has been imposed on them wherever they are found, except under a covenant with Allah and a covenant with men, and they have become deserving of wrath from Allah, and humiliation is made to cleave to them. This is because they disbelieved in the verses of Allah and slew the prophets unjustly. This is because they disobeyed and exceeded the limits. (3.112) They are not all alike. Among the People of the Book there is an upright nation; they recite Allah's verses in the nighttime, falling prostrate; (3.113) They believe in Allah and the Last Day; they enjoin what is right and forbid what is wrong; and they hasten to good works. Those are among the righteous. (3.114) Whatever good they do, they shall not be denied it. Allah knows the pious. (3.115)

This is not a nation of blood relatives or people of a particular ethnicity. It consists of those individuals who enjoin what is right, forbid what is wrong, and believe in God. These are the qualities that make anyone who acquires them a member of the "best nation." This special nation doesn't include only people of the Qur'an, but also followers of Books that God had revealed to previous Prophets, such as the Torah of Moses and the Injīl of Jesus. This is another verse that describes the pious Jews and Christians as a nation:

> Had they observed the Torah, the Injīl, and what was sent down to them from their Lord, they would have eaten both what was above them and what was beneath their feet. Some of them are a just nation; but many of them bad is what they do. (5.66)

The Qur'anic concept of "best nation" shows that piety is the only criterion that differentiates between people in God's sight. This differentiation does not discriminate against people *in this world* by, for example, giving the best nation more rights than others. It only promises them rewards *on the Day of Resurrection*. It does not give them any special privileges in this world. The Qur'an doesn't discriminate between people on the basis of their ethnicity, color, social status, or wealth. No such criteria are used in the Qur'an to prefer some people over others or identify *chosen individuals or groups*. The Qur'an states that people can be better or worse than others, but only on the basis of their behavior:

> O you people! Surely, We have created you of a male and a female and made you peoples and tribes that you may know each other. Certainly, the most honorable of you in the sight of Allah is the most pious of you. Surely, Allah is Knowing, Aware. (49.13)

The Qur'anic concept of "best nation" is completely different from the Old Testament's concept of "chosen people of God" that it applies exclusively to the children of prophet Jacob. The Qur'an says that God *preferred the Israelites above all people* (2.47, 7.140), but this refers to the fact that they were privileged for a long time with being the hosts of many prophets. As we have explained in our book *The Mystery of Israel in Ancient Egypt*, the Biblical presentation of the Children of Israel as God's chosen people amounts to the "Israelization of religion" and is incompatible with the teachings of the Qur'an (Fatoohi & Al-Dargazelli, 2008: 75-79).

Is Christianity More Peaceful Than Islam?

The concept of armed jihad reflects the Qur'an's typical extraordinary honesty and direct approach. Yet this virtue has been used against the Qur'an by some who claim that their religion or philosophy is totally peaceful or at least more peaceful than the Qur'an, meaning that the Qur'an is excessive in its tolerance of the use of violence. We have already seen that the latter suggestion is untrue. As for the former claim, it is simply a fallacy. To dogmatically commit to non-violence regardless of circumstances is a short-sighted position that lacks any sense of realism and reflects astounding ignorance of history and the world. It is also a false commitment whose adherents are forced to abandon it under certain circumstances.

I will deal with these claims using the specific case of Christianity. One reason for this choice is that it is the *most popular* religion that is claimed to give peace a *special* position. The second reason is that it is mainly in countries where Christianity is the predominant faith that

Islam has been misrepresented as a religion of violence. This image is then often contrasted with the supposedly special religion of peace that Christianity represents to show that the latter is a superior faith. I will show that this portrayal of Christianity fails the tests of its teachings and the history of its followers.

Christianity is often promoted as a *totally* peaceful religion that categorically rejects all forms of violence. Its commitment to peaceful methods, it is claimed, is unconditional and uncompromising. In support of this image, reference is often made to an injunction that the Gospels of Matthew and Luke (6:29) attribute to Jesus whereby he instructs the Christian to return violence with more submission, turning his left cheek to the person who strikes him on his right cheek:

> Ye have heard that it hath been said, An eye for an eye, and a tooth for a tooth: But I say unto you, That ye resist not evil: but whosoever shall smite thee on thy right cheek, turn to him the other also. (Matt. 5:38-39)

But contrast those words with the following words which are also attributed to Jesus yet one hardly hear them quoted:

> Think not that I am come to send peace on earth: I came not to send peace, but a sword. For I am come to set a man at variance against his father, and the daughter against her mother, and the daughter in law against her mother in law. And a man's foes shall be they of his own household. (Matt. 10:34-36)

This does not mean that Jesus promoted domestic violence. Similarly, the previous saying is not intended to suggest that the Christian cannot get involved in legitimate violence at all. In both cases, Jesus' words are symbolic.

Muslim scholar Jamal Badawi makes a very interesting point about the prominence of peace in the life of Muhammad and Jesus. He notes that most scholars think that the ministry of Jesus lasted for about three years only. Thus, we have evidence of Jesus Christ following a completely peaceful policy for three years. Badawi points out that Prophet Muhammad's policy was also completely peaceful not only for the first three years of his mission, but for the following eleven as well! As I have already mentioned, Prophet Muhammad and his followers had to deal peacefully with all forms of persecution they were subjected to for fourteen years before they were granted permission to fight back.

Some may argue that Jesus' surrender to crucifixion represents a unique form of peaceful attitude. But this argument has multiple problems. **First**, by the time of the crucifixion, Jesus had a very small following that could do nothing about any hostility toward their leader.

Second, there is no reliable historical evidence that Jesus was actually crucified (Fatoohi, 2008). **Third**, the concept of a suffering Messiah is unhistorical and was introduced by Christians. The Jewish Messiah was supposed to be victorious not get humiliated (Fatoohi, 2009). But even those who believe Jesus was crucified accept that he and his followers were in no position to defend him anyway. In fact, his disciples are reported to have fled and abandoned him after his arrest!

Furthermore, the Christian faith is not based on the New Testament only, but on the Old Testament as well. Unlike the life of Jesus in the New Testament, the lives of the Old Testament prophets contained a great deal of violence. A number of those prophets are portrayed as warriors who fought many battles. For instance, the Old Testament states that Abraham led an army and "smote" his enemy (Gen. 14:15). King David is described as someone who "shed blood abundantly" and "made great wars":

> And David said to Solomon, My son, as for me, it was in my mind to build an house unto the name of the Lord my God: But the word of the Lord came to me, saying, Thou hast shed blood abundantly, and hast made great wars: thou shalt not build an house unto my name, because thou hast shed much blood upon the earth in my sight. Behold, a son shall be born to thee, who shall be a man of rest; and I will give him rest from all his enemies round about: for his name shall be Solomon, and I will give peace and quietness unto Israel in his days. (1 Chr. 22:7-9)

It is true that, unlike the Old Testament, the New Testament does not contain instances of support for violence. For instance, unlike his Jewish counterpart who is a royal warrior, the Christian Messiah is completely peaceful. Even his establishment of the kingdom of God on earth is claimed to happen without violence (Fatoohi, 2009). But it is still misleading to claim that Christianity gives special prominence to peace. It cannot have more of a claim to peace than the Old Testament which it considers as a divine book. Also, accepting the Old Testament as the Word of God means to accept that God has commanded prophets and righteous people to resort to violence in certain circumstances.

The Old Testament aside, other aspects of Christian thought, though non-scriptural, also undermine the positioning of Christianity as *the* religion of peace. Christians have always known all too well that responding to violence with peace only can be unrealistic, unwise, and impractical. This fact was *openly* and *formally* acknowledged as early as four centuries after Jesus Christ by St. Augustine (354-430 CE), one of the most influential Christian thinkers of all time. He introduced the concept of "just war" to complement the "peaceful" nature of

Christianity. This has allowed the convenience of claiming that Christianity is a *totally peaceful* religion while at the same time permitting its followers to resort to war when they deem it just and necessary!

Compare this opportunistic and contradictory presentation of the alleged special status of peace in Christianity with the consistent and realistic approach to the concepts of peace and war in the Qur'an.

Not only the teachings of Christianity, but its history of also rejects the claim that it is particularly associated with peace. The attitude of Christianity, or more accurately some of its representatives, toward peace and war cannot be properly assessed without referring to the crusades. These were certainly *religious* wars that were instigated and supported by Popes and clerics and were carried out under the name of Jesus and Christianity. Pope Urban II (1088-1099 CE), whose speech at the Council of Clermont in November of 1095 effectively launched the first crusade and set in action this deadly chain of religious wars, promised the immediate remission of all sins of anyone who took part in the crusade. Although the crusaders were supposed to target Muslims, their long list of victims included many thousands of Jews and even non-Catholic Christians!

Commenting on a massacre which took place at the end of the first crusade, Karen Armstrong (2002) wrote:

> On July 15 1099, the crusaders from western Europe conquered Jerusalem, falling upon its Jewish and Muslim inhabitants like the avenging angels from the Apocalypse. In a massacre that makes September 11 look puny in comparison, some 40,000 people were slaughtered in two days. A thriving, populous city had been transformed into a stinking charnel house. Yet in Europe scholar monks hailed this crime against humanity as the greatest event in world history since the crucifixion of Christ.

In vivid, grisly details that send a shiver down the spine, J. Arthur McFall (1999) described in an article in the *Military History* magazine what happened in that massacre and how it was perceived by religious clerics:

> The Crusaders spent at least that night and the next day killing Muslims, including all of those in the al-Aqsa Mosque, where Tancred's banner should have protected them. Not even women and children were spared. The city's Jews sought refuge in their synagogue, only to be burned alive within it by the Crusaders. Raymond of Aguilers reported that he saw "piles of heads, hands and feet" on a walk through the holy city. Men trotted across the bodies and body fragments as if they were a carpet for their convenience. The Europeans also destroyed the monuments to Orthodox Christian saints and the tomb of Abraham.
> There were no recorded instances of rape. The massacre was not insanity

but policy, as stated by Fulcher of Chartres: "They desired that this place, so long contaminated by the superstition of the pagan inhabitants, should be cleansed from their contagion." The Crusaders intended Jerusalem to be a Christian city — and strictly a Latin Christian city. "This is a day the Lord made," wrote Raymond of Aguilers. "We shall rejoice and be glad in it."

The Crusaders cut open the stomachs of the dead because someone said that the Muslims sometimes swallowed their gold to hide it. Later, when the corpses were burned, Crusaders kept watch for the melted gold that they expected to see flowing onto the ground. While the slaughter was still going on, many churchmen and princes assembled for a holy procession. Barefoot, chanting and singing, they walked to the shrine of the Holy Sepulchre through the blood flowing around their feet. Reports that the blood was waist deep are believed to have come from a later misreading of a Bible passage. However, in the official letter "To Lord Paschal, Pope Of The Roman Church, to all the bishops and to the whole Christian people" from "the Archbishop of Pisa, Duke Godfrey, now by the grace of God Defender of the Holy Sepulchre, Raymond, Count of St. Gilles, and the whole army of God," the Crusaders recorded that "in Solomon's Portico and in his Temple our men rode in the blood of the Saracens [Muslims] up to the knees of their horses."

After retreating to the al-Aqsa Mosque, the Muslims surrendered and offered a large ransom to Tancred, who gave them his banner to display over the mosque so that they would not be killed. This agreement was not honored by the crusaders. The historian Raymond of Aguilers is here celebrating the massacre with a quote from the Bible: "This is the day which the Lord hath made; we will rejoice and be glad in it" (Ps. 118:24)!

The characters in this quotation need introducing. Fulcher of Chartres was a French chaplain and chronicler of the first crusade. Daimbert, Archbishop of Pisa, led the Pisan fleet of the campaign. Duke Godfrey, another leader of the crusade, became the first Latin ruler in Palestine after the capture of Jerusalem. He refused the title of "king" preferring to be called "Defender of the Holy Sepulchre." Raymond of Saint-Gilles, Count of Toulouse, was the oldest and most prominent of the crusading princes.

Nothing in the history of Christians suggests that they were more peaceful than other religions and people. The two biggest wars in the history of humanity, World War I and II, which resulted in tens of millions of deaths were started by the Christian world. While, unlike the crusades, these two wars and many other wars that Christians were involved in were not religious, they show that the history of Christians is far from being one of peace — certainly not one of responding to aggression with peace. In the real world, a real slap on a real cheek, even of a Christian person, is very unlikely to produce a Gospel kind of response.

The crusades resulted in massacres on the largest scales. Although these religious wars were blessed, and even instigated, by the highest authorities of the Church, including Popes, the Western media does not associate these acts of genocide with Christianity. Recent conflicts in Europe — in places such as Serbia, Kosovo, and Chechnya — provide many examples of massacres of Muslims by Christians, sometimes involving the silent approval or even explicit support of the Church. None of these are interpreted as meaning that Christianity is a violent religion. The bloody conflict between Catholics and Protestants in Northern Ireland is never attributed to Christianity. The role of the Church in the Rwandan genocide of 1994 has also failed to link the religion of the Church to violence. Such violent conflicts and crimes, unlike ones where the wrongdoers are Muslims, never yield media terms such as "Christian terror," "Christian terrorists," "Christian terrorism," and "militant Christianity."

Similarly, the *religiously driven* Jewish occupation of Palestine, which is supported by various fundamental Christian denominations, and the consequent destitution of its people have failed to generate terms linking Judaism to terrorism.

It would be wrong to ascribe violence committed by some Christians or under the name of their religion to Christianity or link the terror committed by Jewish groups or the Jewish state to Judaism. But it is equally wrong to associate Islam with violence for the misdemeanor of a minority of its followers.

So it is misleading to claim that Christianity is more peaceful than, hence superior to, other religions, such as Islam, that accommodate the use of violence in some circumstances. Such claim is refuted by the teachings of Christianity and the history of some of its followers.

Do you [O you who believe!] think that
you will enter Paradise before Allah has
known those who *jāhadū* (did jihad) and
the patient among you?

(Qur'an, 3.142)

4

Peaceful Jihad: The Permanent Struggle Against the Inner Enemy

This chapter explains peaceful jihad. Unlike its armed counterpart, peaceful jihad has existed since the early days of Islam. It is the permanent form of jihad.

Peaceful Jihad in Meccan Verses

Muslims were given the permission to resort to armed jihad in Medina in the second year after the immigration of the Prophet to that city. Any mention of jihad in verses that were revealed in Mecca must, therefore, refer to peaceful jihad. This means that peaceful jihad existed long before armed jihad.

This is one of the Meccan verses that mention jihad:

> Had it been Our will, We could have sent a warner to every town. (25.51) So do not [O Muhammad!] obey the disbelievers and *jāhidhum* (do jihad against them) with it [the Qur'an] a mighty *jihādan* (jihad). (25.52)

Doing jihad using the Qur'an means preaching its teachings. This is described as jihad because it involves a *struggle* against the disbelievers who would resist, often violently, the new religion. It also involves personal struggle on the part of the Prophet who would have to force himself to accept the suffering that this duty puts him through.

Verse 29.6 is another Meccan verse that speaks about jihad:

> Whoever hopes to meet Allah, the term appointed by Allah will surely come. He is the Hearing, the Knowing. (29.5) Whoever *jāhada* (does jihad), he *yujāhidu* (does jihad) only for his own soul. Surely, Allah is in no need for people. (29.6) [As for] those who believe and do good works, We shall certainly remit from them their bad works, and We shall certainly reward them according to the best of their past deeds. (29.7)

Both verses that surround verse 29.6 talk about the righteous people, indicating their behaviors represent jihad. Jihad is the way of life that brings the person nearer to God.

The term jihad in the Meccan verses 29.69 and 16.110 also denotes peaceful jihad specifically:

> Who does greater wrong than he who forges lies against Allah or denies the truth when it has come to him? Is Hell not the [fitting] abode for the disbelievers? (29.68) As to those who *jāhadū* (did jihad) for Us, We shall certainly guide them to Our ways. Allah is surely with the doers of good. (29.69)

> Those (the disbelievers) are they on whose hearts, hearing, and eyes Allah has set a seal, and those are the heedless ones. (16.108) No doubt that in the hereafter they will be the losers. (16.109) As to those who immigrated after they were persecuted, then *jāhadū* (did jihad), and were patient, then surely your Lord [O Muhammad!] after that will be Forgiving, Merciful. (16.110)

Because of the mention of the immigration, verse 16.110 is considered by some scholars to have been revealed in Medina even though it occurs in a Meccan chapter, as there are instances of Medinite verses in Meccan chapters and vice versa. However, we know that some Muslims did migrate from Mecca before the Prophet left it, so the verse could be referring to those immigrants. What favors this interpretation is describing those immigrants as having followed up their immigration with adhering to patience, which is likely to mean that their flights occurred before the permission to fight back was granted.

Obviously, jihad is not only about fighting in the cause of Islam. Peaceful jihad is actually by far the most common form of jihad in the life of the Muslim. Before the revelation of the verse that granted the early Muslims permission to armed jihad, they were involved in peaceful jihad only. For about fourteen years peaceful jihad was the only form of jihad in the life of the early Muslims.

Aspects of Peaceful Jihad

Peaceful jihad includes each and every effort that the person who embraces Islam makes in order to change himself to what God wants him to be. Behaving as a true Muslim means giving up personal and social evil habits and practices; resisting bad desires; sharing with the poor; helping the needy; being patient, forgiving, fair, kind, compassionate ....etc. All these aspects of good behavior are forms of peaceful jihad. Peaceful jihad is the struggle against the bad qualities and drives of the lower self.

This form of jihad also includes every peaceful effort to change others and the world for the best. For instance, spreading the message of the Qur'an and the values of Islam — such as justice, compassion, and forgiveness — is peaceful jihad. Peaceful jihad is what the life of the Muslim is all about, as he/she must be in continuous struggle against evil, whether inside him/her or in the external world.

Throughout the Qur'an, God urges the Muslims to combine "faith" and "good works." The expression "those who believe and do good works" and its variants occur tens of times in the Qur'an. The term "good works" is almost synonymous with the term "jihad," though each emphasizes different aspects of those deeds. The term "jihad" stresses the fact that these deeds are not things that the human is naturally inclined to or easily accepts, so the emphasis is on the *struggle* involved. For instance, making a habit of donating one's money and giving it to the needy, rather than using it to seek personal pleasures and worldly riches, is not something that the person naturally feels comfortable with. So, this form of "good works" is jihad.

At the same time, this kind of behavior benefits the charitable individual spiritually and psychologically, the recipients of that help, and, ultimately, society as a whole. Most acts of peaceful jihad have other beneficiaries in addition to the acting Muslim himself. The Qur'an describes these actions with an Arabic term, *ṣāliḥ*, that may also be translated as "righteous," in addition to "good." This description is derived from the fact that these actions *put right* flaws in individuals and society.

The Qur'an contains so many verses that do not mention the word "jihad" explicitly but still teach aspects of peaceful jihad. This is an example:

> Successful indeed are the believers, (23.1) who are humble in fear in their prayers; (23.2) who keep away from vain talk; (23.3) who pay the obligatory alms; (23.4) who guard their private parts, (23.5) except before their spouses or those whom their right hands possess, in which case they won't be blameworthy, (23.6) but whoever seeks to go beyond that, these are the transgressors; (23.7) who observe their trusts and covenant; (23.8) who keep up their prayers. (23.9)

These verses detail some of the attributes of the true believer, teaching Muslims what they need to do. Every effort to emulate those attributes is an act of peaceful jihad. All those actions involve some form of struggle to overcome the resistance of the lower self. Naturally, different actions of jihad involve different degrees of struggle. Let's go through the verses above on peaceful jihad in some detail.

The Muslim is required to pray five times a day as a compulsory duty, but is also required to do extra prayers and remember God until He becomes on his mind almost all the time. Verse 23.2 talks about praying to God with fear and veneration. This is not easy as it is much easier to lose concentration and continue the prayer while absent-minded.

The next verse commands the Muslim not to get engaged in useless conversations that might harm him spiritually. This, again, is not as easy as it may sound. It is difficult to resist the temptation to get involved in all kinds of useless talk that carries no intellectual value and may lead to harm. Note that this is not a command to prevent the Muslims from debating with people who don't share their belief. The Qur'an throughout encourages Muslims to debate and establish dialogue with non-Muslims, as in verse 16.125 (p. 46).

Verse 23.4 then describes the believer as someone who helps the poor and the needy and pays their due. Spending one's money to help others is another difficult action that goes against our instinctive selfishness. Depending on circumstances, this payment can be substantial. When the early Muslims emigrated from Mecca, losing in the course of doing so all of their possessions and wealth, the Muslims of Medina shared happily with their immigrant brethren.

Verses 23.5-7 command the believer to adhere to sexual chastity and have sex only with legitimate partners. Sex is one of the strongest instincts and biological drives, so controlling it is bound to involve inner struggle against the lower self. This is even more so today where sexual references and symbols are almost everywhere.

In the next verse, the believer is described as someone who observes what he is entrusted with and keeps his covenants. At the time of the revelation of the Qur'an and for a long time afterward, people used to entrust each other with their belongings, for instance when they traveled. That common practice was the equivalent of one of today's essential storage and banking services. In those days, trust used to play a greater role in people's dealings with each other, hence God's reference to it in several verses. But where is the struggle involved in this? It is the trustee's resistance to the temptation not to return the belongings he was entrusted with. Equally tempting would be denying a verbal agreement for the sake of illegitimate profits. Resisting such temptations is peaceful jihad. Observing the trust and keeping the promise are good works that promote moral values in society.

Even before the revelation of the Qur'an, Prophet Muhammad was known to the Meccans as *aṣ-Ṣādiq al-Amīn* or "the truthful, the trustworthy." People used to entrust him with their belongings. When the Prophet had to flee Mecca to Medina, he asked his cousin and closest follower 'Alī bin Abī Ṭālib to stay in Mecca to return to people their trusts before joining him in Medina.

Finally, God describes the believers in verse 23.9 as "those who keep up their prayers." Note that He didn't simply say "those who pray." "Praying" is a lot easier a duty than "keeping up prayers." The latter means *consistency* and *continuity* in observing the praying duties. It takes struggle, for instance, to resist the temptation to stay in bed and do the prayer of dawn later in the morning instead of waking up everyday for the prayer before sunrise.

The following two verses mention a number of acts of peaceful jihad that God attributes to the "*muttaqīn*" — a plural term that may be translated as "dutiful," "Allah-fearing," or, as I have done in this book, "pious":

> Those who spend [in the way of Allah] in ease and in adversity, restrain [their] anger, and pardon people. Allah loves the doers of good. (3.134) Those who when they commit an indecency or wrong themselves remember Allah and ask forgiveness for their sins — and who forgives sins save Allah? — and will not knowingly repeat what they did. (3.135)

Even at times of affluence, it is difficult to give one's own money to someone else in need instead of saving it or using it to enjoy one's self. What God orders those who seek His pleasure is even harder. He wants us to spend on those who are in bigger need even when we ourselves are in some need. At such times, we tend to become a lot more apprehensive about the future and fear the worst. God wants us to rely on Him, put those fears behind us, and not allow difficult circumstances to keep us from helping the needy.

God ends verse 3.134 by saying that "Allah loves the doers of good," describing those qualities as good. He encourages us to buy His love with the money that we give to the poor and the needy, by restraining our anger, and by showing forgiveness to those who mistreat us. We have already seen the latter attribute mentioned in verse 42.37 which describes the believers as those who "when they get angry they forgive."

Verse 3.135 emphasizes another aspect of the behavior of the true believers: their readiness and willingness to acknowledge the sins they commit, ask for forgiveness, and desist from committing them. Those sinful acts derive from motives and desires that try to steer the person away from the path of God. It is the persistent and successful resistance to those drives that peaceful jihad is all about.

The word "jihad" does not occur in any of the verses I have quoted from chapters 23 and 3. The acts those verses describe, nevertheless, are all patterns of peaceful jihad. These are forms of struggle that the Muslim has to engage in from day one of recognizing his Islamic identity, accepting that life must not be led arbitrarily, and adopting the Islamic way of life. The verses above talk about everyday challenges, which is why peaceful jihad is an essential aspect of the life of the Muslim. Peaceful Jihad is the process of realizing one's Islamic identify.

The War Against the Lower Self

Peaceful jihad is the quality control that the Qur'an has put in place to ensure that the true Muslim, as opposed to the person who is Muslim only in name, acquire very high qualities.

Many would be surprised to know that jihad is not only about fighting, and that peaceful jihad — which covers all peaceful efforts to oppose evil and promote good — is a form of jihad that is far more present in the Muslim's life than armed jihad. Many more would be astonished to learn that one major form of peaceful jihad is an ongoing war against the enemy *within* the person. This enemy is the lower self. It is this particular enemy, not an external one, that poses the greatest threat to the person's wellbeing.

A very aggressive external enemy whose threat cannot be fended off can turn killer, causing the physical death of his victim. But regardless of his power, means, and aggression, he would be completely incapable of causing the spiritual death of that victim. Killing an innocent person is, in fact, a serious threat to the spiritual wellbeing of the murderer himself, not the victim. The murderer is a deadly external enemy as far as the victim is concerned, but he is still a substantially more dangerous internal enemy as far as himself is concerned. The murderer might well see his successful execution of a crime as a victory of some sort, but it is in reality a complete and disastrous personal defeat.

The enemy within is far more dangerous than anyone without, because it can cause the person's spiritual demise, the ultimate death. Many physically living people are spiritually dead because they are in a state of surrender to their lower selves and refusal to fight them. The Qur'an states that it is one's own sins that could make him ultimately a loser who ends up in Hell, and that it is for those sins repentance is required. These sins are the making of the lower self — that is, the inner rather than an outer enemy.

It should have become perfectly clear by now that peaceful jihad has a much greater presence and role in the life of the Muslim than armed jihad. The Muslim is required to always be in a state of peaceful jihad because no matter how good a Muslim is, there would always be more spiritual diseases to treat and more refinement to do to the soul to bring it nearer to its Creator. The Muslim must remain in a state of jihad against the enemy inside him until he dies. Only then, this peaceful war should come to an end.

Armed jihad is the Muslim's last resort to live in peace with others. That peace he needs for his unrelenting peaceful war against his lower self and evil in the world. Armed jihad's function is to pave the way for peaceful jihad. This may not be what some think, but it is the conclusion from the Qur'an.

The Qur'an does not teach the killing of non-Muslims. Conversely, it portrays non-Muslims as targets for the peaceful efforts to preach the truth of Islam. The Muslim resorts to armed jihad when his right to choose his preferred faith and teach it is eroded by violent and deadly means. The ultimate aim of armed jihad is to create the free and tolerant environment necessary for peaceful jihad.

Peaceful Jihad in Prophetic Sayings

The authenticity of the sayings and doings attributed to Prophet Muhammad, known as "hadith (plural: ahadith)," has always been the subject of disagreement among Muslim scholars. The hadith literature is full of inauthentic sayings that were attributed to the Prophet by different people for a variety of purposes. This is why I have focused on the Qur'an in this book. With this in mind, I would still like to quote some Prophetic sayings that mirror the Qur'anic concept of jihad and emphasize the centrality of peaceful jihad in the life of the Muslim.

Upon returning from one battle, the Messenger of God said to his companions: "We have returned from the lesser jihad to the greater jihad." The Prophet's reference to the jihad that they had returned from was clear to the companions, but some could not understand what he meant by "the greater jihad." When asked about that term, he replied: "The servant's jihad against his desire" (al-'Asqalānī, undated)! In another version the Prophet is reported to have replied: "The Jihad of the heart" (Qārī, undated).

In the entry for the word *juhd* in his book on the glossary of the Qur'an, al-Aṣfahānī (undated) says that the Prophet has said: "Do jihad against your lower drives as you do jihad against your enemies." He is also reported to have said: "Do jihad against your lower selves with hunger and thirst (i.e. by fasting)" (As-Sabkī, undated).

The *Musnad of Ahmad* (undated: 24678) attributes to Prophet Muhammad these words: "The *Mujāhid* (the person who does jihad) is he who does jihad against his lower self in obeying Allah, the Mighty, the Sublime."

In another succinct hadith that urges the Muslim to kill his lower self before he faces physical death, the Prophet is reported to have said: "Die before you die" (az-Zarqānī, undated).

If they incline to peace then incline [O
Muhammad!] to it, and rely on Allah.
Surely, He is the Hearing, the Knowing.
(Qur'an, 8.61)

5

Misreading the Qur'anic Term of "Jihad"

Misinterpreting and misrepresenting jihad as being about armed jihad only ignores occurrences of the term "jihad" in verses where it can only mean peaceful jihad, as in the Meccan verses (pp. 55-56). This common misunderstanding indicates also the misreading of references to jihad in Medinite verses as meaning armed jihad when they actually mean jihad in general, both armed and peaceful. Let's examine how this can happen.

The Erroneous Reduction of Jihad to Armed Jihad

The early Muslims were almost continuously at war, i.e. involved in armed jihad, with enemies of the new religion from the second year of the immigration of the Prophet to Medina. That particular period witnessed the revelation of most of the verses that mention jihad. To be more precise, twenty four of the thirty verses that contain one variation or another of the term "jihad" were revealed in Medina. (Appendix A lists all verses that contain any variation of the term jihad and the place of revelation of each verse.) This has been commonly taken to mean that the word jihad and its variations in *all* of those twenty four Medinite verses denote armed jihad specifically. This is a serious misinterpretation.

There is a simple reason for the appearance of the term jihad more in Medinite than in Meccan chapters. In Medina, jihad took the *additional* form of armed jihad — something that had an enormous impact on the life of Muslims as individuals and as a community. Armed jihad was crucial in establishing Islam itself and building its base of converts, as it provided the early and future followers of the religion with the freedom and security they needed to practice it. Muslims' engagement in armed jihad was vital for the survival of their religion and, of course, their own survival.

Armed jihad does not involve a struggle against external enemies only, but also a great deal of struggle against the lower self. The ongoing obligatory duty of armed jihad put the Muslims face to face with death for the sake of their religion — an enormous test that they could have chosen to bypass by simply abandoning their faith. Muslims needed a great deal of support and help from God to succeed in their armed jihad on both external and internal fronts. They needed divine help to defeat their much larger and better equipped external enemies. They were equally in need of God's support to defeat their inner enemies: their lower selves. The lower self would try to weaken the Muslim's determination to adhere to his religion and offer all sacrifices needed. These sacrifices could be as substantial as involving one's possessions or even one's life. The lower self would find him excuses as to why he shouldn't get involved in armed jihad.

The help that Muslims needed to overcome the weaknesses that could emerge inside them at such difficult times came partially in the form of additional strength that God bestowed on them. Another form of the divine support was Qur'anic verses praising those who partake in armed jihad and promising them good and at the same time warning against the failure to discharge that important religious duty. This is why the term jihad is mentioned in the Medinite chapters four times more than the Meccan ones.

Even though fighting was common in the life of the Arabs then, armed jihad was a totally different experience. Arabs before Islam used to fight to gain worldly riches, exact revenge on their enemies, defend their property, or defend themselves. Fighting for the sake of God, which is what armed jihad is about, was not something they were accustomed to. It is not only that armed jihad was not about worldly spoils, but it also required from the Muslim sacrifices in both life and property. This is the ultimate sacrifice that merited the help Muslims got partly in the shape of many verses on jihad:

> Say [O Muhammad!]: "If your fathers, sons, brothers, spouses, clans, property that you have acquired, trade whose decline you fear, and dwellings that you like are dearer to you than Allah, His Messenger, and *jihādin* (jihad) in His way, then wait until Allah brings about His command." Allah does not guide the backsliders. (9.24)

One important fact is that even in the Medinite verses, jihad refers to both armed and peaceful jihad. Let's first look at some sample verses:

> Those who believed, immigrated, and *jāhadū* (did jihad) in the way of Allah with their property and selves are much higher in degree with Allah. These are the winners. (9.20)

> *Jāhidū* (do jihad) [O you who believe!] in the way of Allah *jihādihi* (the kind of jihad that is due to Him). He has chosen you and has not laid upon you a hardship in religion; it is the faith of your father Abraham. He [Allah] has named you *al-Muslimīn* (the Muslims) earlier and in this (the Qur'an), so that the Messenger be a witness over you, and you be witnesses over people. Therefore keep up prayer, pay the obligatory alms, and hold fast to Allah. He is your Master; so how excellent a Master and how excellent a Supporter! (22.78)

> O you who believe! Be pious to Allah, seek means of nearness to Him, and *Jāhidū* (do jihad) in His way that you may succeed. (5.35)

Such Medinite verses talk about jihad in general. There is no reason to suggest that they denote only fighting in the way of God.

Some Medinite verses do clearly mention jihad in the context of talking about particular instances of armed jihad. For example, the following verse talks about Muslims who asked the Prophet for permission not to take part in armed jihad:

> Those who believe in Allah and the Last Day do not ask you [O Muhammad!] that they do not *yujāhidū* (do jihad) with their property and selves. Allah is aware of the pious. (9.44)

The following verse mentions Muslims who chose not to join fellow Muslims in their armed jihad and didn't go with their brethren to battle:

> Those who were left behind were glad to sit at home and not join the Messenger of Allah. They were reluctant to *yujāhidū* (do jihad) with their property and selves and said [to other Muslims]: "Do not go forth in the heat." Say [O Muhammad!]: "The fire of Hell is far hotter," if they understand. (9.81)

Verse 9.86 below refers to well-off Muslims who sought permission from the Prophet not to take part in armed jihad. Verse 9.88 contrasts this attitude with the jihad of the Prophet and those who believed with him:

> When a chapter is revealed, stating: "Believe in Allah and *jāhidū* (do jihad) with His Messenger," the wealthy among them (the Muslims) ask permission of you [O Muhammad!] and say: "Let us be with those who sit at home." (9.86) They are content to be with those who stayed home, and a seal is set on their hearts so they do not understand. (9.87) But the Messenger and those who believe with him *jāhadū* (did jihad) with their property and selves. It is these who shall have good things, and it is these who are the successful. (9.88)

Below, verse 9.73 clearly refers to armed jihad by the Prophet and Muslims against disbelievers and hypocrites who betrayed the Muslims and sought unsuccessfully to harm them:

> O Prophet! *Jāhidi* (do jihad) against the disbelievers and the hypocrites and be stern against them; their abode shall be Hell — an evil destiny. (9.73) They swear by Allah that they did not speak [evil], but they certainly did speak the word of infidelity, disbelieved after they embraced Islam, and set out to do that which they failed to attain. They did not hold grudge except because Allah and His Messenger enriched them out of His grace. If they repent, therefore, it will be good for them; and if they turn away, Allah will punish them with a painful punishment in this world and the hereafter, and they shall not have on earth any close friend or helper. (9.74)

These verses mention the term jihad in the context of talking about particular events of armed jihad, but this still doesn't mean that jihad is reduced to armed jihad in those verses. The failure to fight in a battle is a failure to do "armed jihad" and, ultimately, a failure to take part in "jihad" as a whole — the Qur'anic term for both armed and peaceful jihad. The Qur'an does not use two different terms for peaceful jihad and armed jihad. The term covers both types of jihad, but in certain contexts it emphasizes more peaceful jihad, as in the Meccan verses on jihad, and in other contexts it stresses more armed jihad, as in *some* of the Medinite verses.

The Distinction Between Jihad and Qitāl (Fighting)

As we have already seen, jihad is a lot more than fighting in the way of God. The latter is referred to in the Qur'an with the Arabic term "qitāl," which literally means "fighting." Confusing the terms "jihad" and "qitāl" has been influential in the prevalent misreading of all occurrences of jihad in the Medinite verses as references to armed jihad. "Jihad" and "qitāl" have significantly different meanings and uses in the Qur'an.

Qitāl is only one, though the most prominent, aspect of armed jihad (pp. 25-27). The latter is a wider concept that includes every effort involved in both the preparation and execution of war, such as funding it. Armed jihad, in turn, is one form of the broader concept of jihad that involves peaceful jihad also. While it is always true to describe "fighting in the way of God" as "jihad," the opposite is not necessarily true as jihad can also refer to other aspects of armed jihad or to peaceful jihad. This is why the references to "jihad" in the Qur'an cannot be equated with "qitāl."

Particularly helpful in dispelling the widespread confusion of jihad and fighting are the following verses:

> Fighting has been *ordained* on you [O you who believe!], and it is an object of dislike to you; and it may be that you dislike a thing while it is good for you, and it may be that you love a thing while it is evil for you; and Allah knows whereas you do not know. (2.216)

> Have you not seen [O Muhammad!] those to whom it was said: "Withhold your hands [from fighting], keep up prayer, and pay the obligatory alms," when fighting was *ordained* on them, a party of them feared people as they ought to fear Allah or [even] with a greater fear, and said: "Our Lord! Why have You *ordained* fighting on us? If You have only granted us a delay to a near date?" Say [O Muhammad!]: "The provision of this world is short, and the hereafter is better for he who acts dutifully toward Allah; and you shall not be wronged in the very least." (4.77)

These verses make it absolutely clear that fighting in the way of God started only when it was "ordained (*kutiba*)" on the believers. Fighting in the way of God is not a practice that comes by default with religion. This description equally applies to fighting in the way of God that previous prophets and their followers were involved in, as shown in the following verse:

> Have you not considered [O Muhammad!] how the chiefs of the Children of Israel who came after Moses said to a prophet of theirs: "Set up for us a king and we will fight in the way of Allah"? He said: "May it be that you would not fight if fighting was *ordained* on you?" They said: "Why would we not fight in the way of Allah having been driven out of our homes, and for the sake of our children?" But when fighting was *ordained* on them, they turned away except a few of them, and Allah knows the wrongdoers. (2.246)

The word "jihad" is never used in a similar way in the Qur'an. There is no verse indicating that jihad was "ordained" at some point before which there was no jihad. This confirms my observation that it is qitāl, not jihad, that denotes fighting in the way of God and which was made a duty on the Muslims in the second year after the immigration to Medina. Significantly, the verse that, at some point, granted permission to the Muslims to use armed jihad (22.39) also talks about *fighting* rather than *jihad*.

Note that verse 9.86 which was quoted earlier in the chapter is not an exception from the conclusion above:

> When a chapter is revealed, stating: "Believe in Allah and *jāhidū* (do jihad) with His Messenger," the wealthy among them (the Muslims) ask permission of you [O Muhammad!] and say: "Let us be with those who sit at home." (9.86)

Obviously, this verse does not mean that "belief in God" and "jihad" would have been first imposed as a duty in the particular chapter that the verse mentions. In fact, the verse does not refer to one particular chapter, but to every chapter that urges the Muslims to do jihad with the Prophet. This verse contrasts this repeated emphasis with the failing of some Muslims to obey the command.

If "qitāl," not "jihad," is the term that specifies fighting in the way of God and "jihad" signifies something more general, then one would expect "qitāl" to be mentioned more than "jihad" in the Medinite chapters. This is indeed the case, with "qitāl" occurring manyfold more than "jihad."

Call [O Muhammad!] to the way of your Lord with wisdom and goodly exhortation and argue with them in the best manner. Surely, your Lord best knows those who go astray from His path, and He best knows those who follow the right way.

(Qur'an, 16.125)

6

Jihad Today

Jihad is a fundamental practice of the journey to God. While this Arabic term has become famous for its use in the Qur'an, the concept would have been mentioned in every divine Book and would have been inspired to every prophet. Jihad is as valid and essential today as it was at the time of the revelation of the Qur'an fourteen centuries ago and at the time of the earlier prophets. Proper understanding of this concept is necessary not only for understanding the history of Islam, but also Islam itself. Jihad is the Islamic way of life, hence its relevance to the life of every Muslim everywhere at any time.

In this chapter, I will highlight negative effects that the misconception of jihad has had and discuss how to apply this Qur'anic concept properly in the world today.

The Essentiality of Jihad

Peaceful jihad is the approach, attitude, mindset, and practice that ensure that the Muslim is in continuous progress toward the ideal state of man: perfect servanthood to God. The failure to recognize peaceful jihad as the *main*, let alone *one*, form of jihad is bound to reflect negatively on the soul and character of the Muslim and his spiritual journey. Such failure indicates the person's willingness to cohabit with various bad qualities.

The mere acceptance of God as the one Lord and Muhammad as His Messenger without trying to apply jihad would not be enough to purify the person spiritually. Every Muslim is bound to be tested by God to see whether he would apply jihad or not:

Do you [O you who believe!] think that you will enter Paradise before Allah has known those who *jāhadū* (did jihad) and the patient among you? (3.142)

Do you [O you who believe!] think that you will be left alone without Allah knowing those of you who *jāhadū* (did jihad) and did not take adherents other than Allah, His Messenger, and the believers? Allah is aware of what you do. (9.16)

We shall try you [O you who believe!] until We know *al-mujāhidīna* (those who do jihad) and the patient among you and test your tidings. (47.31)

Like verse 4.95, which we quoted earlier, verse 9.19 confirms that doing jihad is far superior to any religious ritual. The Quraysh used to provide pilgrims to Mecca with drinking water and look after the Ka'ba, so the verse tells them that this is nowhere as good as having proper faith and practicing jihad:

> Do you [O people!] consider giving drink to pilgrims and tending the Inviolable Mosque as equal to the work of he who believes in Allah and the Last Day and *jāhada* (does jihad) in the way of Allah? They are not equal in the sight of Allah. Allah does not guide the wrongdoers. (9.19)

Those who are Muslims in name only can do considerably more damage to the public image of Islam than an outright enemy. No misbehavior of any number of Muslims can change the truth of Islam, but many people develop ill-informed views of Islam when observing such misdeeds. If Muslims can be so ignorant about Islam, then it should come as no surprise that non-Muslims know more distorting myths than facts about this great religion, with Muslims being the main source of such myths.

The prevailing unawareness of peaceful jihad resulted in the Qur'anic concept of jihad being equated with fighting in the way of God. This misconception was precipitated by an equally important mistake of equating non-equals, this time including the terms "jihad" and "qitāl." When this confusion is coupled with the Qur'anic message that jihad is a permanent duty on the Muslim, it becomes inevitable to conclude that fighting in the way of God is a timeless duty. The consequences of this misguided conclusion are made even worse by the misunderstanding of the rules governing fighting in the way of God. Jihad ends up being erroneously reduced to fighting in the way of God, and the conditions under which such fighting becomes permissible are also misunderstood.

This compound recipe of confusion and misunderstanding is behind the widespread abuse of jihad and the interchangeable use of the concepts of jihad and fighting in the way of God. One form of the abuse of these concepts has been portraying them as the means to enforce an Islamic state. This view of jihad and fighting in the way of God has no foundations in the Qur'an. This particularly dangerous misconception has played in the hands of militants who dream of leading that Islamic state. The name of Islam is thus fully utilized to cater for personal ambitions. Such distortion and making false arguments for personal interests are no different from what politicians and militants of various backgrounds and affiliations have done everywhere in the world.

Those who don't know the true meaning of jihad, let alone practice it, can never create a proper Islamic state. They may take control of a country and start applying what they consider to be Islamic law, as happened in Afghanistan, for instance. Contrary to what they believe, this does not turn that country into an Islamic state. A leader who is ignorant of what jihad is may well fail even to rule with justice, never mind set up an Islamic state. An Islamic state is a state of the highest standards which can be founded only by people who possess both knowledge and piety and uphold the human values of the Qur'an. Proper understanding and application of jihad are essential for the Muslim before he can provide genuine Islamic leadership.

One important point that should be made clear here is that while jihad requires a degree of understanding of Islamic thought, scholarly study of Islam is no substitute for jihad. Islamic scholarship does not guarantee that a scholar is a true Muslim. An Islamic educational institute might graduate scholars in various fields of Islamic thought, but those graduates would not be by default practicing jihad, in the Qur'anic sense of the word. Seeking knowledge is a major duty on the Muslim, but putting that knowledge into practice is the ultimate aim.

A knowledgeable scholar who is short of jihad is like someone who worked hard to gain knowledge just to waste what he earned. The rulings of such a person are likely to be influenced as much by his undisciplined and uncontrolled lower self as by his knowledge. This scholar cannot provide sound and trusted leadership. A quick look at the atrocities and injustice committed in supposedly Islamic states confirms this. One only needs to remember the numerous terrified Muslims who had to flee their supposedly Islamic states seeking refuge in non-Islamic states.

There have been, and perhaps will always be, countries that claim to be "Islamic." These are simply countries whose population is mostly Muslims and which apply a legal system that reflects a particular doctrinal interpretation of Islam. The neglect of basic human rights in such countries confirms that they are far from applying Islam. Rather than serving Islam, as these states claim, they often do the most damage to the image of Islam. Those who do not know much about Islam are likely to form a view about it through the examples set by such states. The reality is that there is no true Islamic state anywhere on this planet today.

Those who dream up an Islamic state often call on the early history of Islam to validate their argument. In the course of doing so, they overlook fundamental differences between the history they cite and the one they try to create. It is true, of course, that the Prophet established what can be described as an Islamic state. But before hastening to draw conclusions from this, we need to remember some critical facts.

First, it was the Prophet himself, the perfect Muslim, who founded the state. **Second**, the creation of that state was a byproduct of the evolvement of great Muslim individuals, not the other way around. It is significant that the Meccan verses focused on the process of developing the individual, whereas it was Medina that later witnessed the revelation of the relatively large number of verses that regulated the affairs of the emerging Islamic community.

Third, the population of the first Islamic state *willingly chose* to join it as they took the Prophet as their leader and the religion that he delivered as their constitution. Muhammad did not impose his leadership on any unwilling population like modern dictatorial hopefuls who want to establish Islamic states often do.

Fourth, historical events and circumstances cannot simply be copied to be recreated in a totally different era. Those who fail to recognize this basic fact are certainly incapable of creating and leading a state, Islamic or otherwise. They try to apply their misunderstanding of the Qur'an and Islamic history to a world that they have equally misunderstood.

Islamic Retaliation to Aggression

Another result of misunderstanding the concept of fighting in the way of God is illustrated in the way some Muslims react to aggression, falling in the trap of responding to evil with evil. In modern times, Muslims have constituted the vast majority of persecution victims where the persecutors and the persecuted belonged to different religions. Many major instances of genocide in the last century saw Muslims forced to play the victims. If the suffering of Muslim populations at the hand of their European colonists is now old history, the massacring of Muslims in places such as Bosnia, Chechnya, and Kosovo is very much recent history. Some of the crimes against Muslim populations, such as in Palestine and Kashmir, have been going on for decades now under the watchful eyes of the world. The wars on Afghanistan and Iraq are the latest additions to this bloody record.

There are always excuses to justify mass murders and acts of genocide; man can find justifications even for the worst and most evil acts. The fact that the religion of the victims of these atrocities is not always specifically the target of the persecution does not change the fact that the victims share the Islamic faith. Also, it is untrue to suggest that the religion of the victims was not on the mind of some of those aggressors as they planned and carried out the crimes. But this is not the right place to discuss why and how Muslims have been targeted. I will focus here on the response of Muslims to some of those atrocities.

The term "jihad" has been used by Muslim individuals and groups to describe their equally atrocious vengeful retaliations to atrocities committed against them or other Muslims. Suicide bombing is one such method that has become popular among some militant groups, even though suicide and indiscriminate killing are both totally rejected by Islam. From the Qur'anic perspective, such reactions violate clear Qur'anic commands that prohibit the Muslims from responding to unjust aggression with the same. I have quoted earlier a number of such verses (5.2, 2.190-2.193) including this one:

> O you who believe! Stand firm for Allah, [as] witnesses with justice. Let not hatred of a people cause you not to act equitably; act equitably; that is nearer to piety. Be pious to Allah. Surely, Allah is aware of what you do. (5.8)

Crimes against Muslims must not be allowed to turn Muslims into criminals. Jihad, and ultimately Islam itself, is here to control the drives to commit evil, even if it is reaction to evil. While indiscriminate and uncontrolled responses to crimes against Muslims are themselves crimes in equal measure, calling those evil acts "jihad" is a crime against Islam. Muslims who behave in this way are far from serving Islam. They do the name of Islam a big disservice while serving only their lower selves.

Muslims must protect fellow Muslims and any victims against aggression. They must also try to bring the aggressors to justice. But Muslims must never allow those evil people to turn them into similar criminals. If Muslims fail to adhere to the principles of the Qur'an when reacting to the victimization of Muslims, they would simply help their enemies in achieving their goals. They would be siding with their enemies against themselves.

Furthermore, Muslims must not support those who are in the wrong even if they are fellow Muslims:

> Help one another in [practicing] righteousness and piety, and do not help one another in [committing] sin and transgression. Be pious to Allah. Surely, Allah is severe in punishment. (from 5.2)

Some Muslims teach proudly and confidently that Muslims should help their brethren and defend them whether they are right or wrong. This goes against the teachings of the Qur'an. There a number of verses, like 5.2, that make it clear that that Muslims must take the right side, even if that meant standing up to fellow Muslims.

"Islamic" Violence or "Western" Double Standards?

Some Muslims do not adhere to the Qur'anic principles when responding to injustices and violence that they or fellow Muslims are subjected to. At times, they make innocent victims pay for the aggressors' crimes. This form of injustice has been committed by Muslims and non-Muslims alike. History of ancient and modern violent conflicts, involving various cultures and religions, confirms that this is a universal phenomenon. When a violent aggressor is powerful and immune to retaliation, the frustration, desperation, and rage of the victims can at times make them inflict their violent revenge on innocent, vulnerable people whose only crime is some association with the aggressor, even though they had nothing to do with the aggressor's crimes.

One aspect of the problem of the violent image of Islam in the West is the focus on the violent reactions of some Muslims while almost completely ignoring the miseries that pushed them down that road. It is right to condemn Muslims', and to that matter any party's, violent behavior that targets innocent people. But failing to acknowledge and denounce the violence that Muslims suffered and resulted in their violent reaction is equally criminal and condemnable. The modern term for this is "double standards."

Applying double standards in any conflict can guarantee only one thing: claiming more innocent victims on all sides. I do not think those who apply double standards in a conflict can be separated from the culprits. They share the responsibility for any blood shed, child orphaned, family rendered destitute, and atrocity committed. As I was driven to write this book by the tragedies of September 11, I would like to cite an incident to show the use of double standards and their damaging effects.

In the middle of December 2001, TV channels and radio stations across the world broadcasted excerpts from a video tape by Osama Bin Laden. In the one hour long tape, the terrorist calls the attack of September 11 "blessed," and talks at length about his version of "jihad" against the West. He cited instances of Western injustices against Muslims in various regions in the world as a justification for his and his followers' war against the USA and the West. He talked about the mass killing of innocent Palestinians, the death of more than half a million children in Iraq as a result of the sanctions, the persecution of Muslims in Kashmir, and other tragedies. What we are particularly interested in here is the comments that this speech drew from Western politicians.

The White House spokesman dismissed the speech as "nothing more than the same kind of terrorist propaganda we've heard before." "Terrorist propaganda" is how the Israeli Foreign Ministry spokesman also described it. The other comment that Western politicians rallied to make is that the tape proved Bin Laden's involvement in the criminal attack of September 11, 2001. As put by the British Foreign Secretary: "By boasting about his involvement in the evil attacks, Bin Laden confirms his guilt."

At first glance, the response of the Western politicians might seem reasonable and understandable. After all, they exposed Bin Laden's tape as "terrorist propaganda" and, thus, neutralized any effect it could have. The reality, though, is that this response was nothing but a complete failure to deal with the real issue that this tape raised. The politicians' response amounted to a non-response.

The reason that the reaction of Western politicians was effectively a non-response is quite simple and straightforward. Bin Laden cited the persecution and suffering of Muslims in some countries and accused the West of being heavily involved in those tragedies in order to urge Muslims to attack the West and Western interests everywhere. Bin Laden was not that stupid to try to recruit the average Londoner, Californian, or Berliner for his bloody cause. He was addressing and trying to move *Muslims* who were experiencing or following closely the years-long injustices that he mentioned. Yet the response of Western politicians, was to tell *Westerners* who did not care or know much about those ongoing tragedies that Bin Laden's tape was "terrorist propaganda"!

What those Westerners thought of the tape, if they had time to listen to or read excerpts from it, was irrelevant. It is what Muslims, the overwhelming majority of whom do not live in the West, made of his speech that really mattered. Particularly important to the West should have been the response of those Muslims who can be vulnerable to Bin Laden's rhetoric. This audience was completely ignored by the unwise politicians in the West. I cannot think of a better endorsement Bin Laden could have had from Western politicians for his message. They proved his point for him.

Bin Laden used what is described in Arabic as a "right argument for a false purpose." He incited hatred against the USA and the West in general by citing their involvement in sufferings of Muslims to ask his audience to join his campaign of brutal terror. Western politicians chose to address Westerners because they can easily overlook the facts that Bin Laden cites in front of an audience that listens only to Western media or knows little about the problems that Bin Laden mentions. They ignored the target audience of Bin Laden's message because they cannot come up with any convincing response to an audience that is well-informed on these issues, let alone people who have been living those injustices.

Western politicians could not explain why more than half a million Iraqi children had to die because of sanctions that they imposed to punish a brutal dictator who the West decided one day to demonize and change his identity from friend to foe. They were unable to explain why a whole people in Palestine should be driven out of their homes and forced to live for generations in camps under humiliating and brutal occupation forces that the West has boastfully supported and misleadingly portrayed.

This incident happened shortly after the terrorist attacks on the USA, but several similar incidents have since happened. Bin Laden's later tapes talked about more recent problems, such as the devastating wars in Iraq and Afghanistan, to stir up the feelings of his target audience. He used new facts but he did not change his goal. The politicians in the West also chose not to change their failure to respond to him.

By choosing not to respond to Bin Laden's recruitment message, Western politicians chose yet again to apply double standards. We are back to square one and the vicious circle goes on. Muslims are left to continue to suffer away from the eyes of the rest of the world. Some would feel an urge to inflict misery on the West to exact revenge and/or bring a change. Innocent, vulnerable victims are then caught up by the bloody rage. Here is another proof on the violence of Islam and Muslims, we are then told!

There is another dishonest but popular tactic that is used by Western politicians and media to avoid facing up to what really drives some Muslims to terrorism. It is the claim that Bin Laden and his likes wage their terror campaigns because they want to destroy the Western values and way of life! As I argued in my article on *The London Bombings and the Double Identity Crisis of Britain and the British Muslim*:

> The suicide bombers in Palestine have been killing themselves and Israelis not because they do not like the Israeli lifestyle. Bin Laden and his followers never said that they bombed and will continue to bomb America because the American electoral college system is not to their liking. The terror that is infesting Iraq now is not the result of the terrorists' objection to the democratization of Iraq. Similarly, the Leeds terrorists did not blow themselves and tens of people up simply to protest against our food, drink, cinemas, and other aspects of our lifestyle. None of these and similar terror groups were formed and continue to operate around the agenda of *changing the British or American way of life*. (Fatoohi, 2005)

The reality is that what drives Bin Laden and other terrorists is grievances in Muslim countries that the West has got, one way or another, involved in. These grievances are no justification for atrocities, but the persistent refusal to acknowledge the real causes of this terror is no less evil or devastating.

Muslims in Present Day Conflicts

Muslims need to recognize that the world they live in today has barely any resemblance to the world at the time of Prophet Muhammad. Today's world is immeasurably more complicated. Modern conflicts and challenges, therefore, are also often more complex than those of the far past.

In the wars in which the early Muslims were involved, differentiating between the good and the evil parties was straightforward. Prophet Muhammad and his followers wanted only to follow their faith. The disbelievers did not only decide not to embrace Islam, in which case no problem would have occurred, but they also brutally persecuted Muslims. This aggression was the cause of the wars that broke out between Muslims and their enemies.

Many Muslims tend to classify any war between Muslims and non-Muslims as a war between good and evil, right and wrong, faith and infidelity. Consequently, they classify the fighting of Muslims as armed jihad, though they use the general term "jihad." This simple model of classifying warring parties and identifying the case for armed jihad applied perfectly to the wars that the early Muslims were involved in. Then, the peace seeking Muslims stood for what is right and good while their aggressive enemies represented what is wrong and evil. This is why God granted Muslims the right to armed jihad in the first place (pp. 31-32):

> Permission [to fight] has been granted to those against whom war is waged, because they are oppressed. Surely, Allah is well capable of assisting them [to victory]. (22.39) [The permission is to] those who have been driven out of their homes without a just cause, only because they say: "Our Lord is Allah." Had it not been for Allah's repelling some people by means of others, then certainly cloisters, churches, synagogues, and mosques in which Allah's name is much remembered would have been pulled down. Surely, Allah will help him who helps His cause. Surely, Allah is Mighty, Invincible. (22.40)

But even then, not every violent aggression by disbelievers against Muslims necessarily counted as a cause for armed jihad. For instance, as I have pointed out in my comment on verse 8.72 (pp. 37-38), an aggression by disbelievers against Muslims who did not immigrate to Medina did not count as a cause for armed jihad for the Muslims of Medina if those disbelievers had a peace treaty with the Prophet:

> Surely, those who believed, immigrated, and *jāhadū* [did jihad] with their property and selves in the way of Allah and those who gave shelter [to the immigrants] and helped them are guardians of each other. As for those who believed but did not immigrate, you [O you who believe!] have no duty of guardianship toward them until they immigrate. If they seek help from you for

the purpose of religion, then help is incumbent on you, except helping them against a people with whom you have a treaty. Allah sees what you do. (8.72)

This is a clear-cut case where violent religious persecution of some Muslims by non-Muslims was differentiated from the case of aggression against the Muslims of Medina, hence did not call for armed jihad. Given the far more complicated nature of today's violent conflicts, there is even more reason not to hasten and liken modern armed conflicts between Muslims and non-Muslims to the wars that Prophet Muhammad and the early Muslims fought against the disbelievers. In fact, we can read warnings of such complication to come in the Qur'an itself as it talks about inter-Muslim conflicts:

If two parties of the believers fought one another, mediate [O you who believe!] between them. But if one of them acted wrongfully toward the other, fight the party that acts wrongfully until it returns to Allah's command. Then if it returns, mediate between them with justice and act equitably. Surely, Allah loves the equitable. (49.9)

This verse talks about a war between two factions of Muslims. God here orders the other Muslims to mediate between the warring parties and broker a peace. If one faction then rejected the reconciliation and peace and insisted on fighting unjustly, then neutral Muslims are ordered to fight those aggressors. The principle underlying this divine command is very simple and straightforward. By rejecting peace and insisting on their unjust war, those Muslims would have acted exactly like the disbelievers who launched unjust war against Muslims. Should the war against those in the wrong convince them to stop their aggression, Muslims must mediate between the two warring parties and find a peaceful resolution for the conflict.

The verse highlights the fact that Muslims can be on the wrong side of a conflict. In fact, they can go astray to the extent of unjustly fighting other Muslims that other Muslims, as instructed by the Qur'an, would have to fight them.

A number of conflicts in recent times have involved Muslims fighting each other, with other Muslims being victimized by the wars. This is one way of looking, for example, at the Iran-Iraq war in the 1980s, and the violent history of Afghanistan after the expulsion of the occupying Soviet army. It is also true that some of those conflicts involved various non-Muslim groups each fighting alongside the warring parties or at least providing them with various forms of support. Throughout their eight-year long war, both Iraq and Iran were aided by Western governments and intelligence agencies that they publicly denounced as national enemies or even enemies of Islam. In such situations, it is simply impossible to say that the party that is fighting a just war is the Muslims and the wrongful side is the non-Muslims. Both warring sides were Muslims, and both were supported by non-Muslims. If this situation is not complicated enough, a war may involve more than two warring parties each of which includes people of different affiliations. This is particularly true of civil wars, such as Afghanistan's, the one that broke out several times between Kurdish parties in Northern Iraq after the Gulf war in 1991, and the more recent civil war between Sunnis and Shias in Iraq after the 2003 invasion and occupation.

One essential condition for applying armed jihad is the availability of clear evidence of aggression by one party against another. This is not the case in many of today's complicated conflicts. Let's remember the following verse:

> O you who believe! When you travel in the way of Allah, investigate and do not say to someone who offers you peace: "You are not a believer," seeking riches of this world, for with Allah there are abundant spoils. You too were so before, then Allah conferred favors on you. So investigate. Allah is aware of what you do. (4.94)

Note the emphasis that God puts on seeking evidence before taking action. The Muslim must not resort to armed jihad before being absolutely sure that peace is not an option and that fighting is fully justified. If there is any doubt as to whether there is a case for armed jihad, then the Muslim must not carry out any armed action until all doubts are addressed and he has become totally certain that armed jihad is justified and the only solution. The Prophet extended this Qur'anic ruling to the civil penal system also, ordering Muslims not to apply the legal punishment when there is any doubt about the conviction: "Suspend the application of the punishments prescribed by the Law whenever there are doubts." He is also reported to have said to 'Alī bin Abī Ṭālib "O 'Alī! Give evidence only on something [that is clear] like this," and he pointed to the sun, meaning that Alī should not give convicting evidence unless he is completely certain (al-Jilani, 2008: 152).

I have already noted that one major reason for the ease with which some Muslims declare armed jihad is the widespread misunderstanding of jihad in general and armed jihad in particular. One equally influential factor is the underestimation of the high status of peace in the Qur'an.

Qur'anic Peace and the World Today

The Qur'an makes it clear that the state of war between the early Muslims and their enemies was started by the latter. I quoted earlier a number of verses that promote peace and encourage the Muslims to respond immediately and positively to the first signs of the enemy becoming interested in peace (pp. 33-37). That is the position that the Qur'an taught Muslims to adopt in an era and place where peace did not command much respect. While the Qur'an injected genuine love of peace into the Muslims, the interest of their enemies in peace was mainly pragmatic. Nevertheless, Muslims had to stretch out a hand of peace toward their enemies once the latter showed interest in peace. Significantly, there are verses that indicate that the Muslims used to make peace even with enemies who repeatedly broke their word.

God ordered the early Muslims to seek peace at a time when peace lovers were few and far between. No question, there is much more appreciation of peace today, not the least because of the awareness of the increasing degree of destruction that modern wars can cause. There has not been a modern armed conflict where peace seekers could not be found on all sides. This is a sign of optimism in a world that is depressing with its level of aggression and violence. The followers of the Qur'an have to make the most of this growing inclination toward peace. This is a great time to put the Qur'anic message of peace into practice.

The increasing interest in peace means that people are more willing to talk even to their sworn enemy. This is also a great opportunity for Muslims. The Prophet used to negotiate with his enemies and that he would stop talking to them only when they wouldn't be willing to negotiate anymore. It is time to quote this great verse again:

> Call [O Muhammad!] to the way of your Lord with wisdom and goodly exhortation and argue with them in the best manner. Surely, your Lord best knows those who go astray from His path, and He best knows those who follow the right way. (16.125)

Talks and negotiations are far more valued today than by the illiterate, semi-savage population of the Arabian Peninsula at the time of the Messenger. Given God's command to the Prophet above, today's Muslims are required to continuously engage in dialogue with other people, including their enemies. The Qur'an stresses that patience, endurance, tolerance, and, particularly, responding to evil with good can turn an enemy into a close friend:

> The good work and the evil work are not equal. [O Muhammad!] Repel [evil] with the best response, then the person between you and whom there is enmity would become like a close friend. (41.34) No one will receive it (this grace) but those who exercise patience, and no one will receive it but he who has great fortune. (41.35)

Responding to evil with good requires patience. Forcing one's self to behave in this way involves a great deal of jihad. The fruit of this jihad, which is converting enemies into friends, is so great in the sight of God that He describes those who get it as having "great fortune."

The Qur'an was the guide of the Prophet in his debates with people (16.125). All Muslims must seek inspiration from this unique Book. Muslims believe that the Qur'an is the greatest miracle, but many of them don't treat it in a way that reflects this belief. This divine peaceful weapon can achieve results no other weaponry can. Man-made weapons can allow Muslims to kill their persecutors and oppressors. The Qur'an, on the other hand, can instead make Muslims win over many of those enemies or at least convince them that they can all live in peace. By teaching the true message of the Qur'an and applying it, Muslims should be able to make peace with many of their enemies before they get to the point where using arms to defend themselves is the only option left. This is real victory. This is a miracle that only the Qur'an can work.

During the time of the Prophet, there were disbelievers who wouldn't accept to live in peace with Muslims, leaving the latter with no other option but to fight them. However, other enemies who were ultimately won over and who chose to convert to Islam were manyfold more than those who were killed. This is one miracle of the Qur'an.

Despite the intensive hostile propaganda, Islam is the fastest growing religion today, with many people converting to it all the time. These numbers can be even higher if Muslims can better utilize the great power of the Qur'an. The degree of success of the enemies of Islam in distorting its image is indicative of the extent of the failure of Muslims to present the truth of their religion to the world.

We have not sent you [O Muhammad!]
but as a mercy to the worlds.

(Qur'an, 21.107)

7

The Reality of Jihad

We have studied jihad in the Qur'an and examined how peaceful and armed jihad were conducted at the time of Prophet Muhammad. Our conclusions are substantially different from the common views of jihad. The concept of jihad in the Qur'an is clearly at odds with its popular images, including those held by many Muslims. In fact, the propagation of distorted images of jihad should be credited in no small measure to Muslims who are ignorant of the teachings of the Qur'an — the Book of Islam and the main source of its thought.

The *genuine* misunderstandings identified in this book have two main causes. **First**, the inadequate attention given to studying and understanding the Qur'an. **Second**, overemphasizing other religious and historical sources which can be described at best as secondary and at worst as inauthentic and misleading. Unlike other studies, this book has presented a purely Qur'anic study of jihad.

The concept of Jihad, and Islam in general, has also been the target of *deliberate* misrepresentation. This has been the work of a West that used to see Islam as a threat to its interests and values and Muslim individuals and groups who used Islam to advance their non-Islamic ambitions. Western double standards have also played a major role in distorting Islam.

Let's summarize our main findings. **First**, distorting the image of Islam is not a recent phenomenon. Countries that today represent the "West" developed and believed in distorted and fancied images of Islam since the early days of this religion. In recent times, powerful media driven by various interests and double standards have made sure that the image of Islam remained distorted in the West. The West has made Islam pay for its conflicts with the Muslim world. In modern times, Muslims' opposition to the West-supported occupation of Palestine has particularly played a major role in the kind of popular image that the West has painted for Islam. This support for the Jewish state is driven by a mix of religious and political motives.

Second, linguistically, the term "jihad" refers to the process of "exerting efforts" to achieve a goal. Some "struggle" or "resistance" is also implied by the term. The term doesn't identify the nature of the effort or the goal. There are two Qur'anic verses in which jihad is used in this generic meaning.

Third, in the other twenty eight verses in which jihad is mentioned, the term is used in the specific meaning of exerting effort in the cause of God. The main form of Qur'anic jihad may be called "peaceful jihad." It includes the struggle against the evil drivers of the most dangerous enemy that lives inside every human being: the lower self. It is a war against the enemy within. It also includes the peaceful efforts to put right anything that is wrong and support good against evil in the world. Unlike armed jihad, which comes into existence only when there is an aggressive, external enemy, peaceful jihad is a permanent aspect of the life of the Muslim.

Fourth, under particular circumstances, Muslims have the right to carry arms to defend themselves against violent aggression. Fighting in the way of God is the most important component of this second form of jihad, which may be called "armed jihad." The Qur'an describes in detail the various aspects of fighting in the way of God, making clear the difference between proper use and abuse of this form of jihad.

Armed jihad is not a blind tool to inflict revenge in retaliation for aggression. Even when victimized, Muslims are told in the Qur'an that they cannot retaliate in whatever way they may feel inclined to. The Qur'an uncompromisingly rejects the concept of responding to injustice, wrongdoing, and aggression with the same. God has allowed Muslims to resort to armed jihad when their lives are threatened and when armed struggle is the only way to save lives. But He has attached many conditions to armed jihad to ensure that it serves the just function it was created for and has made clear what is legal use and what is abuse.

Armed jihad exists for as long as its need exists. Once that need has disappeared, there can be no more armed jihad. Armed jihad is the war that Muslims get involved in to protect themselves against an aggressive, external enemy. As soon as that aggression has ceased, armed jihad ends.

Fifth, there is widespread misunderstanding of the term "jihad" as meaning "fighting in the way of God." This stems from the failure to realize the existence of a peaceful form of jihad and from confusing the two Qur'anic terms of "jihad" and "*qitāl* (fighting)".

The divine command to the Muslims to carry arms to defend themselves in Medina is reflected in the numerous occurrences of the term "qitāl" and its variations in the Medinite chapters. The vital role of fighting in the way of God for the survival of the early Muslims, and thus Islam, explains the emphasis that God put on His command to the Muslims to fight in His cause.

Fighting for the sake of God was bound to spark inside the Muslim a struggle with his lower self. The latter would urge him to choose a safer and more comfortable life. While repeatedly urging the Muslims to fight in His cause, God reminds the Muslims now and then of the wider context of that fighting by commanding them to be involved in jihad. Those references are essential in reminding the Muslim that jihad is what Muslim life is about, and that fighting in His cause happened to be one major aspect of jihad at the time.

Realizing these facts is essential to avoid misreading the term jihad in the Medinite verses as referring to armed jihad only.

Finally, In addition to the ever-needed struggle against the lower self, the jihad that is most needed from the Muslim today is the peaceful jihad to show the real and beautiful image of Islam. There is a fierce but peaceful war to be won against a huge propaganda machine. It is the peaceful battle to spread the true message of Islam and counteract and foil the relentless efforts to distort it not only by non-Muslims, but by Muslims who know little about Islam beyond its name or simply use this religion for their own interests.

The virulent trumpets of misinformation will be silenced one day. In order to make this day come as soon as possible, Muslims need to work hard to teach the truth of Islam. Only peaceful jihad can set truth aside from falsehood. With Muslims being at the heart of many of today's global conflicts, proper understanding of Islam can only make the world a better place for both Muslims and non-Muslims. It is true that there are circumstances when armed jihad is called for, but in today's world, Muslims can achieve a lot more by peaceful jihad.

Jihad is an ongoing struggle against all manifestations of evil. This struggle can only make better individuals and, consequently, a better world. The Qur'an calls on each one of us to do jihad against all forms and roots of evil, but it commands the individual to start first with the enemy within: the lower self and its inferior drives. Coupling this jihad against the lower self with jihad in the outer world to establish the real image of Islam is the true practice of Islam.

Those who believe, the Jews, the
Christians, and the Sabaeans —
whoever believe in Allah and the Last
day and do good — they shall have their
reward from their Lord, and there is no
fear for them nor shall they grieve.

(Qur'an, 5.69)

Appendix A

The Qur'anic Verses That Contain the Term "Jihad"

This appendix provides a complete listing of all verses in which the word "jihad" or one of its variants occurs. I have not included verse 9.79 which contains the word "*juhdahum*" — meaning "their capacity, effort, or labor" — as it is not related to the subject of this study, although that word shares the same root with "jihad."

There are fifteen different linguistic variations of "jihad" in those verses. I have grouped together the verses that contain exactly the same word. The groups are listed in the English alphabetical order of the transliterated variations of the term "jihad" that they contain, ignoring the definite articles in two groups.

There are thirty different verses in total. Verses 29.6, 25.52, 22.78, and 4.95 occur twice each in the listing, as each contains two different forms of the word jihad.

Due to the significance of the place of revelation of the verse, I have indicated it in square brackets at the end of each verse. Only six of these verses were revealed in Mecca. The remaining twenty four verses were all revealed in Medina.

Jāhada

Do you [O people!] consider giving drink to pilgrims and tending the Inviolable Mosque as equal to the work of he who believes in Allah and the Last Day and *jāhada* (does jihad) in the way of Allah? They are not equal in the sight of Allah. Allah does not guide the wrongdoers. (9.19) [Medinite]

Whoever *jāhada* (does jihad), he *yujāhidu* (does jihad) only for his own soul. Surely, Allah is in no need for people. (29.6) [Meccan]

Jāhadāka

We have enjoined on man goodness to his parents, but if they *jāhadāka* (do jihad against you) to make you associate with Me [a god] of which you have no knowledge [being a god], do not obey them. To Me is your return [O people!], so I shall inform you of your past doings. (29.8). [Meccan]

If they *jāhadāka* (do jihad against you) to make you associate with Me [a god] of which you have no knowledge [being a god], do not obey them, but keep kind company with them in this world; and follow the way of he who turns to Me. Then to Me is your return [O people!], then I shall inform you of your past doings. (31.15) [Meccan]

Jāhadū

Surely, those who believed and those who immigrated and *jāhadū* (did jihad) in the way of Allah hope for the mercy of Allah; and Allah is Forgiving, Merciful. (2.218) [Medinite]

Do you [O you who believe!] think that you will enter Paradise before Allah has known those who *jāhadū* (did jihad) and the patient among you? (3.142) [Medinite]

Surely, those who believed, immigrated, and *jāhadū* [did jihad] with their property and selves in the way of Allah and those who gave shelter [to the immigrants] and helped them are guardians of each other. As for those who believed but did not immigrate, you [O you who believe!] have no duty of guardianship toward them until they immigrate. If they seek help from you for the purpose of religion, then help is incumbent on you, except helping them against a people with whom you have a treaty. Allah sees what you do. (8.72) [Medinite]

Those who believed, immigrated, and *jāhadū* (did jihad) in the way of Allah and those who gave shelter [to the immigrants] and helped them are truly the believers. They shall have forgiveness and bountiful provision [from Allah]. (8.74) [Medinite]

Those who believed afterward, immigrated, and *jāhadū* (did jihad) with you [O you who believe!] are of you. Those who are relatives have prior rights to the guardianship of each other in the ordinance of Allah. Surely, Allah knows all things. (8.75) [Medinite]

Do you [O you who believe!] think that you will be left alone without Allah knowing those of you who *jāhadū* (did jihad) and did not take adherents other than Allah, His Messenger, and the believers? Allah is aware of what you do. (9.16) [Medinite]

Those who believed, immigrated, and *jāhadū* (did jihad) in the way of Allah with their property and selves are much higher in degree with Allah. These are the winners. (9.20) [Medinite]

But the Messenger and those who believe with him *jāhadū* (did jihad) with their property and selves. It is these who shall have good things, and it is these who are the successful. (9.88) [Medinite]

As to those who immigrated after they were persecuted, then *jāhadū* (did jihad), and were patient, then surely your Lord [O Muhammad!] after that will be Forgiving, Merciful. (16.110) [Meccan]

As to those who *jāhadū* (did jihad) for Us, We shall certainly guide them to Our ways. Allah is surely with the doers of good. (29.69) [Meccan]

The believers are those who believed in Allah and His Messenger, did not have doubts, and *jāhadū* (did jihad) with their property and selves in the way of Allah. These are the truthful. (49.15) [Medinite]

Jāhidhum

So do not [O Muhammad!] obey the disbelievers and *jāhidhum* (do jihad against them) with it [the Qur'an] a mighty *jihādan* (jihad). (25.52) [Meccan]

Jāhidi

O Prophet! *Jāhidi* (do jihad) against the disbelievers and the hypocrites and be stern against them; their abode shall be Hell — an evil destiny. (9.73) [Medinite]

O Prophet! *Jāhidi* (do jihad) against the disbelievers and the hypocrites and be stern against them; their abode shall be Hell — an evil destiny. (66.9) [Medinite]

Jāhidū

O you who believe! Be pious to Allah, seek means of nearness to Him, and *Jāhidū* (do jihad) in His way that you may succeed. (5.35) [Medinite]

Go forth [O you who believe!] whether you are free or busy, and *Jāhidū* (do jihad) in the way of Allah with your property and selves; that is better for you, if you know. (9.41) [Medinite]

When a chapter is revealed, stating: "Believe in Allah and *jāhidū* (do jihad) with His Messenger," the wealthy among them (the Muslims) ask permission of you [O Muhammad!] and say: "Let us be with those who sit at home." (9.86) [Medinite]

Jāhidū (do jihad) [O you who believe!] in the way of Allah *jihādihi* (the kind of jihad that is due to Him). He has chosen you and has not laid upon you a hardship in religion; it is the faith of your father Abraham. He [Allah] has named you *al-Muslimīn* (the Muslims) earlier and in this (the Qur'an), so that the Messenger be a witness over you, and you be witnesses over people. Therefore keep up prayer, pay the obligatory alms, and hold fast to Allah. He is your Master; so how excellent a Master and how excellent a Supporter! (22.78) [Medinite]

Jihādan

So do not [O Muhammad!] obey the disbelievers and *jāhidhum* (do jihad against them) with it [the Qur'an] a mighty *jihādan* (jihad). (25.52) [Meccan]

O you who believe! Do not take My enemy and your enemy for guardians, offering them love while they have rejected what has come to you of the truth, having driven out the Messenger and you because you believe in Allah, your Lord — if you have gone forth *jihādan* (doing jihad) in My way and seeking My pleasure. You show love to them in private, and I know what you conceal and what you reveal. Whoever of you does this, he indeed has gone astray from the straight path. (60.1) [Medinite]

Jihādihi

Jāhidū (do jihad) [O you who believe!] in the way of Allah *jihādihi* (the kind of jihad that is due to Him). He has chosen you and has not laid upon you a hardship in religion; it is the faith of your father Abraham. He [Allah] has named you *al-Muslimīn* (the Muslims) earlier and in this (the Qur'an), so that the Messenger be a witness over you, and you be witnesses over people. Therefore keep up prayer, pay the obligatory alms, and hold fast to Allah. He is your Master; so how excellent a Master and how excellent a Supporter! (22.78) [Medinite]

Jihādin

Say [O Muhammad!]: "If your fathers, sons, brothers, spouses, clans, property that you have acquired, trade whose decline you fear, and dwellings that you like are dearer to you than Allah, His Messenger, and *jihādin* (jihad) in His way, then wait until Allah brings about His command." Allah does not guide the backsliders. (9.24) [Medinite]

Al-Mujāhidīna

Not equal are the believers who have no impediment yet sit at home and *al-mujāhidūna* (those who do jihad) in the way of Allah with their property and selves. Allah has favored *al-mujāhidīna* (those who do jihad) with their property and selves over those who sit at home with a higher degree; and Allah has promised good to both. Allah has favored *al-mujāhidīna* (those who do jihad) over those who sit at home with a mighty reward. (4.95) [Medinite]

We shall try you [O you who believe!] until We know *al-mujāhidīna* (those who do jihad) and the patient among you and test your tidings. (47.31) [Medinite]

Al-Mujāhidūna

Not equal are the believers who have no impediment yet sit at home and *al-mujāhidūna* (those who do jihad) in the way of Allah with their property and selves. Allah has favored *al-mujāhidīna* (those who do jihad) with their property and selves over those who sit at home with a higher degree; and Allah has promised good to both. Allah has favored *al-mujāhidīna* (those who do jihad) over those who sit at home with a mighty reward. (4.95) [Medinite]

Tujāhidūna

[The best trade is] that you [O you who believe!] believe in Allah and His Messenger and *tujāhidūna* (do jihad) in the way of Allah with your property and selves. That is better for you, if you know. (61.11) [Medinite]

Yujāhidu

Whoever *jāhada* (does jihad), he *yujāhidu* (does jihad) only for his own soul. Surely, Allah is in no need for people. (29.6) [Meccan]

Yujāhidū

Those who believe in Allah and the Last Day do not ask you [O Muhammad!] that they do not *yujāhidū* (do jihad) with their property and selves. Allah is aware of the pious. (9.44) [Medinite]

Those who were left behind were glad to sit at home and not join the Messenger of Allah. They were reluctant to *yujāhidū* (do jihad) with their property and selves and said [to other Muslims]: "Do not go forth in the heat." Say [O Muhammad!]: "The fire of Hell is far hotter," if they understand. (9.81) [Medinite]

Yujāhidūna

O you who believe! Whoever among you turns back from his religion, then Allah will bring a people whom He loves and who love Him; who are humble toward the believers, proud toward the disbelievers, *yujāhidūna* (do jihad) in the way of Allah, and do not fear the blame of any blamer. That is the favor of Allah that He gives to whom He pleases. Allah is All-embracing, Knowing. (5.54) [Medinite]

Muhammad is no more than a
messenger before whom messengers
have already passed away. Should he,
therefore, die or get killed, would you
turn back on your heels? He who turns
back on his heels will not cause Allah
any harm. Allah will reward the grateful.

(Qur'an, 3.144)

Appendix B

A Brief Chronology of the Life of Prophet Muhammad

This is a very brief listing of the dates of major events in the life of Prophet Muhammad. All of these events are referred to in the book.

Date (CE)	Event
570	Birth of the Prophet in Mecca. His father had already died.
575-576	The death of the Prophet's mother.
578	The death of the Prophet's grandfather and custodian 'Abd al-Muṭṭalib. The Prophet's uncle Abū Ṭālib became his guardian.
610	The first revelation of the Qur'an.
612-613	The Prophet started calling people to Islam publicly.
614	The first immigration of Muslims to Abyssinia escaping the persecution of the idol-worshipping Meccans. They stayed there for three months. A second immigration to Abyssinia, involving more Muslims, took place later on. This time, the immigrants stayed in Abyssinia until 628 CE when they rejoined the Prophet in Medina.
615	The tribe of Quraysh imposed economic and social sanctions on Muslims and the clan of Prophet Muhammad, Hāshim.
618-619	The collapse of the sanctions.
618-619	The death of Abū Ṭālib, the Prophet's uncle, triggering increased hostility from the Meccans toward the Prophet.
622	The emigration of the Prophet from Mecca to Medina.
624	The first major battle of the Muslims against the disbelievers, known as the battle of Badr.
630	The Muslims peaceful conquest of Mecca.
632	The last revelation of the Qur'an.
632	The departure of the Prophet from this world in Medina.

References

Al-'Asqalānī, A. (undated) (In Arabic). *Al-Kāfi ash-Shāfi*.

Al-Aṣfahānī, A. (undated) (In Arabic). *Mufradāt al-fādh al-Qur'an*.

Al-Bukhārī, M. (undated) (In Arabic). *Al-Jāmi' al-Musnad aṣ-Ṣaḥīḥ al-Mukhtasar Min Umūr Rasūli Allah was Sunanih was Ayyamih*.

Al-Jilani, A (2008). *Purification of the Mind (Jila' Al-Khatir)*, Luna Plena Publishing: UK.

Armstrong, K. (2001). *Muhammad: A Biography of the Prophet*, Phoenix Press: London.

Armstrong, L. (2002). "The curse of the infidel: A century ago Muslim intellectuals admired the west. Why did we lose their goodwill?" *The Guardian*, June 20.

As-Sabkī, T. (undated) (In Arabic). *Tabaqāt ash-Shafi'iyyah al-Kubrā*.

Az-Zarqānī, M. (undated) (In Arabic). *Mukhtaṣr al-Maqāṣid*.

Fatoohi, L. & Al-Dargazelli, S. (2008). *The Mystery of Israel in Ancient Egypt: The Exodus in the Qur'an, the Old Testament, Archaeological Finds, and Historical Sources*, Luna Plena Publishing: UK.

Fatoohi, L. (2005). "The London Bombings and the Double Identity Crisis of Britain and the British Muslim," *http://www.quranicstudies. com/louay-fatoohi/miscellany/the-london-bombings-and-the-double-identity-crisis-of-britain-and-the-british-muslim.html*.

Fatoohi, L. (2007a). "One Night in a Cave that Changed History Forever" *http://www.quranicstudies.com/louay-fatoohi/quran/one-night-in-a-cave-that-changed-history-forever.html*.

Fatoohi, L. (2007b). *The Mystery of the Historical Jesus: The Messiah in the Qur'an, the Bible, and Historical Sources*, Luna Plena Publishing: UK.

Fatoohi, L. (2007c). *The Prophet Joseph in the Qur'an, the Bible, and Historical Sources: A New Detailed Commentary on the Qur'anic Chapter of Joseph*, Luna Plena Publishing: UK.

Fatoohi, L. (2008). *The Mystery of the Crucifixion: The Attempt to Kill Jesus in the Qur'an, the New Testament, and Historical Sources*, Luna Plena Publishing: UK.

Fatoohi, L. (2009). *The Mystery of the Messiah: Jesus' Messiahship in the Qur'an, the New Testament, the Old Testament, and other Jewish Sources*, Luna Plena Publishing: UK.

Huntington, S. (2002). "The Age of Muslim Wars," *Newsweek*, January.

Lings, M. (2006). *Muhammad: His Life Based on the Earliest Sources*, Inner Traditions Intl Ltd: Vermont.

McFall, J. A. (1999). "Climax of the First Crusade," *Military History*, June.

Qārī, M. A. (undated) (In Arabic). *Al-Asrār al-Marfū'a*.

Southern, R. W. (1978). *Western Views of Islam in the Middle Ages*, Harvard University Press: Massachusetts.

Tisdall, W. C. (1905). *The Original Sources of the Qur'an*, Society For Promoting Christian Knowledge: London.

Index of Qur'anic Verses

2.23-24	17		5.54	91
2.47	48		5.66	47
2.79	18		5.69	46
2.109	40		6.106	44
2.111-112	20		6.107	45
2.119	45		7.140	48
2.127-128	11		8.55	34
2.130-133	20		8.56	34, 35
2.136	21		8.57	34
2.190	39, 40		8.58	34, 35
2.190-2.193	73		8.59	34
2.191	39, 41		8.60	34, 35
2.192	39		8.61	35
2.193	39, 40		8.62	30, 35
2.194	41		8.63	31
2.215	16		8.72	37, 77, 78, 88
2.216	32, 66		8.74-75	88
2.218	88		9.6	36
2.244	25		9.7-9	36, 37
2.246	67		9.10-13	37
2.256	44		9.16	69, 88
2.281	15		9.19	69, 70, 87
2.285	21		9.20	64, 88
3.19-20	20		9.24	64, 90
3.103	30		9.40	29
3.110-115	47		9.41	89
3.123	32		9.44	65, 91
3.134-135	59		9.73	65, 89
3.142	69, 88		9.74	65
4.74	25		9.79	87
4.77	32, 66		9.81	26, 65, 91
4.80	45		9.86	65, 67, 89
4.84	26		9.87	65
4.89	33		9.88	65, 88
4.90-91	34		9.120	26, 33
4.94	42, 43, 79		9.121	26
4.95	32, 69, 87, 90		10.37-38	17
4.125	20		10.72	19
4.145	44		13.7	45
5.2	38, 40, 73		13.40	45
5.8	39, 40, 73		15.9	17
5.13	40		15.94	13, 45
5.35	65, 89		15.95-98	45
5.44	19		16.108-109	56

16.110	55, 56, 88		33.40	21
16.125	46, 58, 80, 81		39.41	45
16.126	41		41.34-35	80
20.130	25		41.41-42	17
22.38	31		42.36	39
22.39	31, 32, 67, 77		42.37	39, 59
22.39-40	33		42.38	39
22.40	31, 32, 77		42.39	39, 40
22.41	31		42.40	39, 40, 41
22.78	19, 64, 87, 89, 90		42.41-42	39, 40
			42.43	39
23.1-3	57		42.48	45
23.4-5	57, 58		43.88-89	44
23.6	57		46.9	21
23.7	57, 58		47.31	69, 90
23.8	57		49.9	78
23.9	57, 58		49.13	48
25.51	55		49.15	26, 88
25.52	55, 87, 89		50.45	45
27.44	21		53.29	45
29.18	45		53.30	45
29.5	55		60.1	33, 89
29.6	55, 87, 91		60.8-9	44
29.7	55		61.11	90
29.8	23, 87		66.9	89
29.68	56		88.21-22	45
29.69	55, 56, 88		93.1-11	16
31.14	23		96.1-5	15
31.15	24, 88		109.1-6	46

Index of Names and Subjects

'Abd al-Muṭṭlib (Prophet Muhammad's grandfather), 11, 93

'Alī bin Abī Ṭālib, 58, 79

Aaron (prophet), 19

Abraham (prophet), 11, 18-21, 50, 51, 64, 89, 90

Abū Bakr, 29

Abū Ṭālib (Prophet Muhammad's uncle), 11, 13, 93

Abyssinia, 13, 93

Adam (prophet), 16, 19

Afghanistan, 42, 71, 72, 76-79

Al-Basūs (war), 35

Arabian Peninsula, 11, 14, 30, 42, 80

Arabs, 14, 17, 21, 26, 30, 41, 64

Archbishop of Pisa (crusader), 52

Armstrong, Karen, 6, 14, 47, 51

atonement, 100

Badr (battle), 32, 93

BBC, 1

Bible, 16, 18, 52

Bin Laden, Osama, 74-76

Bosnia, 72

Buddhists, 46

carpet bombing, 42

Chechnya, 7, 53, 72

Christianity, iii, 5, 6, 13, 46, 49-51, 53, 99

Christians, 20, 46, 47, 50-52

contextual displacement, 18

Council of Clermont, 51

crucifixion, 99, 100

crusaders, 51, 52

crusades, 51, 52

Dāḥis and al-Ghabrā' (war), 36

David (prophet), 18, 19, 50

Day of Judgment, 44, 46

Day of Resurrection, 48

democracy, 1, 3

double standards, 6, 7, 9, 74, 76, 83

Duke Godfrey (crusader), 52

Egypt, 102

Fulcher of Chartres (chaplain), 52

Gabriel (angel), 13

Gulf war, 79

hadith, 3, 61

Ḥamza (Prophet Muhammad's uncle), 36

Hāshim (clan), 11, 13, 14, 93

Hind bint 'Utba, 36

Hindus, 46

Ḥira' (mountain), 12, 13

Holy Sepulchre, 52

holy war, 8, 24, 25

human rights, 1, 32, 33, 71

Huntington, Samuel, 5

Injīl (Jesus' Book), 18, 19, 47

Iran, 78

Iraq, iii, 1, 7, 42, 72, 74, 76, 78, 79

Iraqi-Iranian war, 78

Isaac (prophet), 19-21

Ishmael (prophet), 11, 19, 20, 21

Israel, iii, 7, 48, 50, 67, 95, 99, 102

Jacob (prophet), 19, 20, 21, 48, 103

Jerusalem, 51, 52

Jesus, iii, 13, 16, 18, 19, 21, 47, 49, 50, 51, 95, 99, 100, 101

Jews, 2, 19, 20, 40, 46, 47, 51, 99, 101

John (prophet), 19

Joseph (prophet), 16, 19

Judaism, 5, 46, 53, 99

Ka'ba, 11, 12, 17, 70

Kashmir, 72, 74

Khadīja (Prophet Muhammad's wife, 12, 13

Kosovo, 7, 53, 72

Luke (Gospel), 49

Matthew (Gospel), 49
Mecca, 11-15, 29, 36, 37, 55, 56, 58, 70, 87, 93
Medina (city), 14, 15, 26, 29, 31, 37, 38, 46, 55, 56, 58, 63, 67, 72, 77, 78, 84, 87, 93
Messiah, 50
Middle East, 1
Moses (prophet), 18, 19, 21, 47, 67
New Testament, iii, 18, 50, 95, 99-101
Noah (prophet), 19
Northern Ireland, 53
Old Testament, 18, 50
Palestine, 42, 52, 72, 76, 83
Palestinians, 74
Paul (apostle), 100
People of the Book, 20, 40, 46, 47
polygyny, 12
polytheists, 13, 36, 37, 44, 45
qitāl (fighting), 8, 25-27, 66, 67, 70, 84
Queen of Sheba, 20
Quraysh (tribe), 11, 13, 14, 70, 93
Qurayshites, 14, 36, 40, 46
Ramadhan, 13

Raymond of Aguilers (historian), 51, 52
Raymond, Count of St. Gilles (crusader), 52
Romans, 101
Rushdie, Salman, 6
Rwanda, 53
Sabaeans, 46
Saracens, 52
Saudi Arabia, 11
September 11, 2001, 1, 51, 74, 75
Serbia, 7, 53
Shiasm, 3
Sikhs, 46
Solomon (prophet), 19-21, 50, 52
St. Augustine, 50
suicide bombers, 7
suicide bombing, 7, 73
Sunnism, 3
Syria, 12
Torah, 18, 19, 47
Urban II (Pope), 51
USA, 7, 74-76
weapons of mass destruction, 42
World War I, 52
World War II, 52
Yathrib (city), 13, 14
Zachariah (prophet), 19
Zoroastrians, 46

The Mystery of the Messiah
The Messiahship of Jesus in the Qur'an, New Testament, Old Testament, and Other Sources

• The Messiah in Judaism, Christianity, and Islam

• An Islamic reading of the history of the concept of "Messiah"

• Unhistorical images of the Jewish and Christian Messiahs

• The misrepresentation of the Messiah as king

• The second coming of the Christian Messiah

Publication Date: May 2009

ISBN: 978-1-906342-05-0

Available from Amazon and other bookstores

The Messiah is the central figure of the largest religion in the world, as Christianity was formed around Jesus' messiahship. Judaism also gives the Messiah a special and high position, although it denies that Jesus was the Messiah, so the Jews continue to wait for the coming of their Messiah.

The Qur'an confirms the Christian belief that Jesus was the Messiah, but it has fundamental differences with the Christian representation of the Messiah. Islam has even more differences with the Jewish concept of the Messiah.

This book compares the concept of "Messiah" in Judaism, Christianity, and Islam. It examines the portrayal of the Messiah in the Old Testament and other Jewish writings, the New Testament, and the Qur'an. It develops a complete picture of how this concept appeared, what it originally represented, and how it was changed over time by different believers. The study shows why and how the Messiah was developed in Judaism into a military king whose main role is to re-establish Israel and restore its glory. It also explains how Christianity turned this victorious Jewish warrior into a suffering spiritual king.

The author's ultimate goal is to show that the Qur'anic Messiah is the historical one. Neither a victorious royal with a political agenda nor a defeated spiritual teacher who ended up on the cross, the Messiah was a prophet sent by God. This new critical reading of the history of the "Messiah" challenges deep-rooted prejudices and misunderstandings about this concept.

The Mystery of the Crucifixion
The Attempt to Kill Jesus in the Qur'an, the New Testament, and Historical Sources

- Flaws of the Gospel accounts of the crucifixion

- Does history really support the crucifixion tradition?

- The Qur'an's explanation of the crucifixion

- The origin of the theology of the cross

- The reality of Jesus' appearances after the crucifixion

Publication Date: November 2008
ISBN: 978-1-906342-04-3
Available from Amazon and other bookstores

Numerous books and articles have been published about the crucifixion. Western studies have focused on the Christian narratives and historical sources, but most of them have completely ignored the Qur'an, which denies that Jesus was crucified. Muslim scholars have also studied the Qur'an's account but mostly in exegetical works that focused on the Qur'an's version of the story, with some comparative references to the Gospel narratives but almost no consideration of historical sources.

This book takes a new approach by considering the crucifixion in the Qur'an, Christian writings, and early historical sources. It discusses the serious flaws in the Gospel accounts and the unreliability of the few non-scriptural sources. The book also challenges common modern alternative readings of the history of that event. One new contribution that this study makes to the literature of the crucifixion is its new interpretation of all related Qur'anic verses. It also presents a coherent explanation of the development of the fictitious story of the crucifixion of Jesus.

The theology of the cross that Paul developed is also examined. The book shows that the doctrine of the atonement conflicts with the Gospel teachings and is refuted in the Qur'an.

The Mystery of the Historical Jesus
The Messiah in the Qur'an, the Bible, and Historical Sources

• Jesus in the Qur'an, Christian writings, and historical sources

• The scriptural Jesus in the light of history

• The life and teachings of the historical Jesus

• The time and places in which Jesus lived

• Jesus and the Jews and the Romans

• The historical Jesus versus the theological one

Publication Date: September 2007

ISBN: 978-1-906342-01-2

Available from Amazon and other bookstores

Jesus remains one of the most studied characters in history. In the two millennia since his birth, countless writers have published numerous books and articles on every aspect of his life, personality, teachings, and environment. Depending on the backgrounds, goals, and trainings of their respective authors, these works relied on the New Testament, other Christian sources, Jewish writings, or other historical sources, or on combinations of these writings. The Qur'an is rarely mentioned, let alone seriously considered, by the mainly Christian authors of these studies. This explicit or implicit neglect reflects a presumed historical worthlessness of the Qur'an.

Muslim scholars have also written extensively about Jesus. Contrary to their Western counterparts, they have studied in detail what the Qur'an and other Islamic sources say about Jesus. The Christian image of Jesus is often cited to be dismissed, usually on the basis of what Islamic sources say, but at times also because of its incoherence and inconsistency. Like Western scholars who have ignored the Qur'an, Muslim writers have shown no interest in independent historical sources.

This book fills a gap in the literature on the historical Jesus by taking the unique approach of considering together the Qur'an, the Gospels, and other religious and historical sources. This genuinely new contribution to the scholarship on the historical Jesus shows that, unlike the New Testament accounts, the Qur'anic image of Jesus is both internally consistent and reconcilable with known history. While showing that our understanding of how the New Testament was formed and our growing knowledge of history confirm that the Christian Jesus is unhistorical, this study makes a strong case for the historicity of the Jesus of the Qur'an.

The Mystery of Israel in Ancient Egypt
The Exodus in the Qur'an, the Old Testament, Archaeological Finds, and Historical Sources

- The Israelites in ancient Egypt

- The Qur'anic and Biblical accounts of the exodus

- Historical problems in the Biblical narrative

- The exodus in archaeological finds

- The exodus in historical sources

- Identifying the Pharaoh of the exodus

Publication Date: December 2008
ISBN: 978-1-906342-03-6
Available from Amazon and other bookstores

Few events in history have fascinated the layperson and the scholar as much as the exodus of the Israelites from ancient Egypt. This phenomenal interest has led to extensive research into scriptural, historical, and archaeological sources. The Qur'an, however, has been completely ignored by Western researchers because of the faith put in the Biblical narrative and the prejudiced view that the Qur'an's account is based on Jewish sources, including the Bible.

This book examines in detail the Biblical narrative of the exodus, showing that it contains a substantial amount of inaccurate and false information. It also shows that the similarities between the Qur'anic exodus and its Biblical counterpart are very limited and the differences between the two scriptures are much greater in number and detail. Particularly significant is the fact that the Qur'an is free of the erroneous and inaccurate Biblical statements that have contributed to the rejection of the historicity of the exodus by many scholars. The book demonstrates that the Qur'anic account is consistent with what we know today from archaeological finds and historical sources. This pioneering study is an attempt to create what might be called "Qur'anic archaeology."

The Prophet Joseph in the Qur'an, the Bible, and History
A new, detailed commentary on the Qur'anic Chapter of Joseph

- Modern and comprehensive interpretation of the sūra of Joseph

- Verse by verse analysis and commentary

- Comparative references to classical interpretations

- Comparison between the story in the Qur'an and its Biblical counterpart

- Examination of the historical time and place where Joseph lived

- Explanation of the Qur'an's style in relating history

Publication Date: August 2007

ISBN: 978-1-906342-00-5

Available from Amazon and other bookstores

The Qur'anic sūra (chapter) of Joseph deals almost entirely with the story of this noble Prophet, his brothers, and their father Prophet Jacob. Since the revelation of the Qur'an fourteen centuries ago, there have been numerous attempts to interpret this sūra. The present study is a genuinely new look at the sūra — including careful examination of the historical background of its story and detailed comparison with the corresponding Biblical narrative. While referring to interpretations from classical exegetical works, this book offers new insights into the meanings and magnificence of this Qur'anic text.

The author is not only concerned with analyzing the individual verses; he is equally focused on showing how various verses are interrelated, explicitly and subtly, to form a unique textual unit. He shows particular interest in unveiling subtle references and meanings that are often overlooked or missed by exegetes. Through this comprehensive study, the author elucidates why the Qur'an has always been firmly believed to be a unique book that could have only been inspired by Allah.